MORNING MAKEOVER

HOW TO BOOST YOUR PRODUCTIVITY,
EXPLODE YOUR ENERGY, AND CREATE AN
EXTRAORDINARY LIFE - ONE MORNING AT
A TIME!

DAMON ZAHARIADES

ARTOFPRODUCTIVITY.COM

Art Of Productivity

http://www.artofproductivity.com

❀ Created with Vellum

OTHER BOOKS BY DAMON ZAHARIADES

∾

The Joy Of Imperfection: A Stress-Free Guide To Silencing Your Inner Critic, Conquering Perfectionism, and Becoming The Best Version Of Yourself!

Is perfectionism causing you to feel stressed, irritated, and chronically unhappy? Here's how to silence your inner critic, embrace imperfection, and live without fear!

∾

The Art Of Saying NO: How To Stand Your Ground, Reclaim Your Time And Energy, And Refuse To Be Taken For Granted (Without Feeling Guilty!)

Are you fed up with people taking you for granted? Learn how to set boundaries, stand your ground, and inspire others' respect in the process!

∾

The Procrastination Cure: 21 Proven Tactics For Conquering Your Inner Procrastinator, Mastering Your Time, And Boosting Your Productivity!

Do you struggle with procrastination? Discover how to take quick action, make fast decisions, and finally overcome your inner procrastinator!

~

Fast Focus: A Quick-Start Guide To Mastering Your Attention, Ignoring Distractions, And Getting More Done In Less Time!

Are you constantly distracted? Does your mind wander after just a few minutes? Learn how to develop laser-sharp focus!

~

Small Habits Revolution: 10 Steps To Transforming Your Life Through The Power Of Mini Habits!

Got 5 minutes a day? Use this simple, effective plan for creating any new habit you desire!

~

To-Do List Formula: A Stress-Free Guide To Creating To-Do Lists That Work!

Finally! A step-by-step system for creating to-do lists that'll actually help you to get things done!

~

The 30-Day Productivity Plan: Break The 30 Bad Habits That Are Sabotaging Your Time Management - One Day At A Time!

Need a daily action plan to boost your productivity? This 30-day guide is the solution to your time management woes!

~

The Time Chunking Method: A 10-Step Action Plan For Increasing

Your Productivity

It's one of the most popular time management strategies used today. Double your productivity with this easy 10-step system.

Digital Detox: The Ultimate Guide To Beating Technology Addiction, Cultivating Mindfulness, and Enjoying More Creativity, Inspiration, And Balance In Your Life!

Are you addicted to Facebook and Instagram? Are you obsessed with your phone? Use this simple, step-by-step plan to take a technology vacation!

For a complete list, please visit

http://artofproductivity.com/my-books/

YOUR FREE GIFT

❧

I have a gift for you. It won't cost you a dime. It's a 40-page PDF guide titled *Catapult Your Productivity! The Top 10 Habits You Must Develop To Get More Things Done.* It's short enough to read quickly, but meaty enough to offer actionable advice that can change your life.

I'd like you to have a copy with my compliments.

Claim your copy of *Catapult Your Productivity* by clicking the link below and joining my mailing list:

http://artofproductivity.com/free-gift/

Before we get started, I'd like to say thank you for reading this book. I know your time is limited and you have a lot of options regarding how to spend it. The fact that you've chosen to spend it reading *Morning Makeover* means the world to me.

Again, thank you.

Now, let's dig into how to create morning routines that can literally change your life. I think you're going to be delighted with your decision to go on this adventure!

WISDOM OF THE AGES

∼

"When you arise in the morning, think of what a precious privilege it is to be alive – to breathe, to think, to enjoy, to love." — Marcus Aurelius

∼

"I have retired, but if there's anything that would kill me it is to wake up in the morning not knowing what to do." - Nelson Mandela

∼

"If you win the morning, you win the day." - Unknown

MY LIFE WITHOUT A MORNING ROUTINE

～

There was a time in my life when my mornings followed no pattern at all. I had just quit my corporate job. As a result, I had nowhere to be at 8:00 a.m., and certainly nowhere that required I wear anything more than a t-shirt and shorts.

I took full advantage of the freedom. I woke up without an alarm, usually after 10:00 a.m. I then puttered around for awhile, reading the news, checking out random blogs, and eating breakfast.

Eventually, I showered, brushed my teeth, gathered my gear (laptop, water bottle, etc.), and headed for a local coffeeshop. Sometimes, I left my home at 11:00 a.m. Other times, I left at 1:00 p.m.

In other words, my mornings were a complete waste of time. I had no routine in place.

Worse, the impact of this oversight extended beyond my morning hours. It had a ripple effect on the rest of my day. If I were to describe my disposition in a single word, it would be "lethargic." I lacked energy and motivation. I felt bored and restless.

As you can imagine, my productivity plummeted. Time slipped through my fingers.

I wasn't ignorant about morning routines. Far from it. In fact, I had followed an effective routine prior to quitting my corporate job. I'd wake up at 4:00 a.m., pour myself a cup of coffee, and start compiling and reviewing sales data from the previous day. Then, around 5:30 a.m., I'd jump in the shower, get dressed, and head off to Starbucks to write. I'd spend from 6:00 a.m. to 7:45 a.m. at Starbucks writing, and then head to the office.

My mornings progressed like clockwork. As a result, the volume of work I completed - *important* work, the type that complemented my goals - was massive. At one point, I had hundreds of websites, had written a bestselling book, and wrote a weekly newsletter read by thousands of subscribers. And I was putting in 50 to 60 hours a week at my corporate job.

It's an understatement to say there was a notable difference in my productivity *with* a morning routine and my productivity *without* one.

There was no contest. My mornings were a mess without a routine.

Things are different in my life today. I've created morning routines that energize me, help me to focus, and increase my productivity. For me, these things set the stage for a successful day.

I'll share one of my routines with you later in this book. More importantly, I'll show you how to create routines that help *you* to achieve *your* goals.

Before we go any further, let's talk about the many ways in which having a morning routine will improve your life.

10 WAYS A MORNING ROUTINE WILL IMPROVE YOUR LIFE

~

The benefits you'll experience when you incorporate a morning routine into your daily life are going to be unique to you. Some people find they're more productive throughout the day. Others discover they feel more relaxed and mindful. Still others are surprised to learn that performing a purposeful morning routine makes them feel more energized, confident, and focused.

Most people find, after a week or two, that the thought of waking up no longer depresses them. In fact, they look forward to getting up early because they know their routines are going to help them to experience a successful day.

You're going to experience benefits that will literally transform your life. Here are the 10 ways a morning routine can do so.

#1 - It Will Give Your Day Structure

Following a deliberate and carefully-planned routine each morning will lend more structure to your day. The repetition of your chosen activities (more on this later) will make your morning, as well as the rest of your day, more predictable. This, in turn, will help you to attend to tasks with greater efficiency.

#2 - You'll Experience More Energy

Many morning activities can dramatically increase your energy. And importantly, some will help to ensure your energy levels don't crash mid-morning.

For example, exercising, going for a short walk, and eating a high-protein breakfast will make you feel energized. Some people find that practicing yoga, meditating, and taking a cold shower does the trick.

We'll talk more about designing a quality morning routine in Part II.

#3 - You'll Be Less Susceptible To Decision Fatigue

The more decisions you make, the lower the quality of those decisions. This effect is called decision fatigue.[1] As this type of fatigue sets in, you become less capable of controlling your impulses and making rational choices.

A morning routine minimizes the number of decisions you make in the morning. The activities you choose become habit, precluding the hard task of deciding whether to do them. Making fewer decisions in the morning allows you to conserve your willpower for decision-making during the rest of your day.

#4 - You'll Be More Productive Throughout The Day

You're familiar with this effect from firsthand experience. When your morning starts well, you feel more in control of your day. Part of this feeling is due to having a positive outlook. Part of it is due to having more energy, feeling more excited, and experiencing less stress. And part of it stems from having a firm grasp on what you need to get done throughout the day.

A quality morning routine prepares your mind to deal with the inevitable daily challenges and obstacles that would otherwise derail your productivity.

#5 - You'll Feel Better

Your morning routine will include activities that are healthy for your mind, body, or both. For example, you might start your day with a glass of water, followed by yoga and meditation. Or you might decide to go for a jog immediately after waking, followed by a hot shower and a high-protein breakfast.

Compare these examples to the process most people go through in the morning. They wake up, reach desperately for the snooze button, and go back to sleep. They eventually drag themselves out of bed for a quick shower, a donut or danish, and coffee. Then, they rush to the office or scramble to get their kids ready for school.

No wonder so many people feel fatigued throughout the day!

#6 - You'll Experience Less Stress

You've experienced the stress that accompanies waking up at the last possible moment and rushing to get things done. All of us have. Whether we're trying to get to the office on time, or make sure our kids are ready for school (dressed, lunches prepared, etc.), the flurry of last-minute tasks can cause significant anxiety.

A good morning routine will eliminate the stress. It'll give you plenty of time to address everything that needs your attention. By the time you leave your home, you'll feel as if you're in complete control of your day.

 # 7 - You'll Enjoy A More Positive Mindset

When you have more energy, feel excited and more in control, and experience less stress, it's difficult to have a negative attitude. You'll naturally feel happier. You'll also be more optimistic about what you can accomplish during the day, regardless of the obstacles you might face.

Don't be surprised if your coworkers or family members note the positive change in your disposition. Moreover, don't be surprised if they gravitate toward you; a positive temperament is appealing to others.

 # 8 - You'll Improve Your Health

The activities you choose to do in the morning should support good physical and mental health. Above, I mentioned yoga, meditation, jogging, eating a nutritious breakfast, and drinking water as examples.

That's just scratching the surface. The point is that your morning routine can play a major role in honing both your body and mind. Whether you'd like to lose weight, get into shape, or improve your memory, the activities you pursue will help you to accomplish your goals.

 # 9 - You'll Have Better Focus

When you start the day with a quality morning routine, you'll find that you enjoy a greater sense of clarity. You'll be better able to focus on whatever you need to get done.

Part of this is the result of enjoying more energy. The more energy you have, the easier you'll find it to concentrate.

Part of it is due to feeling healthier and less stressed. When your body feels good and your mind isn't burdened with anxiety, you can more easily stay on task.

Part of it is also due to enjoying better-quality sleep. (We'll talk more about sleep in *Part I: How To Set The Stage For A Successful Morning Routine.*)

#10 - You'll Enjoy A More Purposeful Day

You'll find that your morning routine will lend greater purpose to the rest of your day. You'll feel a stronger connection to the tasks and projects you need to get done. You'll experience greater clarity with regard to the day's most important items and how they complement your long-term goals.

THE ABOVE ISN'T an exhaustive list of the benefits you'll experience when you adopt a good morning routine. Far from it. But they're the most common benefits folks report enjoying when they act with purpose each morning.

Let's now talk about the importance of intentionality in creating and following a quality morning routine.

[1] https://en.wikipedia.org/wiki/Decision_fatigue

THE IMPORTANCE OF INTENTIONALITY

~

Consider the reasons you wake up in the morning. Maybe it's to ensure you arrive at your workplace on time. Perhaps you drag yourself out of bed to make sure your children are ready for school. Or maybe you're a freelancer. You know that staying in bed means you're not working. And *that* means you're not earning money.

These intentions are based on necessity. You act because you feel you *have* to.

For example, if you're habitually late to work, you might get fired. If you fail to get your kids to school on time, their tardiness might negatively affect their grades. If, as a freelancer, you fail to finish projects, you won't get paid for them.

Our intentions are powerful. They can motivate us. They can spur us to do things we might otherwise believe are impossible. But they can also cause us unnecessary stress.

The good news is that you can create any intentions you desire. You're the captain of your ship. You're the director of your life story.

That's important in the context of designing a quality morning routine. It can make the difference between sticking to your routine each morning - and feeling great for doing so! - and allowing your mornings to be filled with dread and anxiety.

I'll use one of my morning routines as an example. (I perform different routines based on what I need to accomplish on a given day.) Here's my typical Sunday:

- **5:30 a.m.** - Wake up
- **5:35 a.m.** - Brush teeth, use the restroom, try to get my hair under control, and get dressed.
- **5:45 a.m.** - Drink 8 oz. of water.
- **5:50 a.m.** - Drive to a local coffee shop.
- **6:00 a.m.** - Order a Cafè Americano (caffeine jumpstarts my brain).
- **6:05 a.m.** - Read articles by writers whose styles I enjoy. Listen to Spanish flamenco guitar music (e.g. Armik, Jesse Cook, etc.) for background music while I read.
- **6:45 a.m.** - Check Amazon sales reports.
- **6:50 a.m.** - Queue Chopin's Prelude in E minor, Op. 28, No. 4. Start writing.

I have a specific intention in mind for this morning routine: preparing myself to write. This intention isn't borne of necessity. It's borne of *passion*. I go to bed on Saturday excited to wake up the next morning and go through my routine because I'm excited to write.

When you act with purpose, you create intentions that are important to you. They excite you. Importantly, they spur you to take action. For example, you no longer scramble each morning after wasting precious time snoozing, checking social media, and watching television. Instead, you set your intention (preferably the night before), which informs your behavior the next morning.

Ideally, your intentions will exhilarate you. You'll look forward to making them happen.

For example, you might create a morning routine designed to help you to lose weight. The thought of reaching your desired weight should thrill you, and influence your behavior accordingly!

You may come up with a routine that'll help you to relax and focus. In this case, finding your center and starting your day free of stress should excite you!

You might develop a routine that'll spur you to start that side business you've been thinking about launching. The prospect of earning a side income, and perhaps even growing the venture into a full-time business, should galvanize you!

My point is that intentionality is a crucial part of creating and maintaining a quality morning routine. The best part is that you're in complete control.

You decide what you'd like to accomplish. Then, *you* create a morning routine that perfectly complements that intention.

Can you see how starting your morning in this manner can positively impact the rest of your day? You'll feel more rested, energized, and focused, all of which will make you more effective.

This concept will become clearer as we progress through *Morning Makeover*. By the time you finish reading this action guide, creating routines that support your intentions will have become second nature to you.

In the next section, I'll describe what you can expect to learn in this book. Fair warning: we have a lot of material to cover. We'll move fast, so having a roadmap will prove invaluable.

WHAT YOU'LL LEARN IN MORNING MAKEOVER

∽

There are four major parts to *Morning Makeover*. If you take a look at the table of contents, you'll notice we're going to cover every important facet of developing and following a quality morning routine. The pieces of the puzzle are organized, in Parts I through IV, in the most intuitive manner possible.

You'll also notice that the material is organized in a way that ensures you'll be able to easily find select pieces for later review. I strongly encourage you to return to this book periodically. You'll find inspiration in the event you confront obstacles, as well as important strategic details regarding how to create and stick to a quality routine.

Below, you'll find a brief overview of what we're going to cover in *Morning Makeover*.

Part I

It's difficult to maintain a successful morning routine if you're tired when you wake up. Most people need eight hours of quality sleep to function well the following day. If they receive less than eight hours, they tend to feel sluggish and fuzzyheaded. They lack focus and motivation. Consequently, they're more likely to hit the snooze button than get out of bed and go through their routines in preparation for their days.

Part I will show you how to experience restful slumber each and every night. There's no secret. As you'll see, it's mostly a matter of planning ahead.

We'll also talk about the benefits of waking up early, and discuss whether doing so is necessary.

Part II

This is where the rubber meets the road. In *Part II*, I'll lay out a 10-step plan for creating a personalized morning routine. You'll learn how to develop routines that complement your intentions and help you to achieve your daily goals. Each step is explained in detail so there's nothing left to chance.

A morning routine is only valuable to the extent that it improves your life. *Part II* will guide you through the process of creating routines that work specifically for **you**.

Part III

Challenges and missteps are inevitable. In fact, they're par for the course whenever you adopt a new habit. In *Part III*, we'll address the most common challenges people experience when they start implementing their morning routines.

You're likely to confront at least a few of the problems covered in this section of *Morning Makeover*. But forewarned is forearmed.

I'll show you how to overcome them so you can make the most of your morning routines and set yourself up for a successful day.

Part IV

One of the best ways to motivate ourselves to take action is to observe how others benefit from taking the same action. Learning about other people's morning routines, and examining how those routines help them to achieve their daily goals, will spur you to create your own rituals.

Part IV details the routines of 10 highly-effective, ultra-successful people. You're no doubt familiar with many of their names. They include entrepreneurs, motivational speakers, venture capitalists, and even a popular cartoonist. You'll learn about the activities they perform each morning, along with their reasons for doing so.

Taking The First Step Of The Rest Of Your Life

I hope you're as excited to press forward through the material in *Morning Makeover* as I was to write it. The tips and strategies described throughout this book have had a profound effect on my life. If you implement them, I'm confident they'll have a similar effect on yours.

In the following section, I'll show you how to make the best use of the advice in this book. The value of *Morning Makeover* is measured by the extent to which it impacts your life. To that end, it's my hope that this book will become one of your most life-enriching resources.

HOW TO USE THIS BOOK TO IMPROVE
YOUR LIFE

∿

When it comes to adopting new habits, action always trumps intention. How many times have you planned to do something, but failed to follow through on those plans? How many times have you read a useful book, and intended to put the information to use only to neglect to do so?

You're not alone. I'm guilty of doing this. Most people are. After all, reading a book is easy. Taking action on the advice it offers requires more effort. It's tempting to do nothing at all even if you're certain the advice will improve your life.

It's my hope that you'll not only read *Morning Makeover*, but also act upon the advice it offers. That's the only way it can have lasting value in your life.

Morning Makeover is written to effect change. It offers tips and strategies for turning your mornings into high-productivity periods that complement your daily goals. Here's what I suggest you do to squeeze maximum value from this book:

First, determine *why* you want to change your current morning routine. Presumably, you believe doing so will yield benefits that'll make the effort worthwhile. Identify those benefits. Be specific.

Second, don't think of this as a lecture. Think of it as a conversation. Even though you and I aren't talking to one another as we might across a coffee table, this is still a dialogue. You might agree with some of the points I make, but disagree with others. That's completely fine. The important thing is that you're engaged with the content enough to take action.

Third, take notes. Write down ideas that resonate with you (or record them online using Evernote). Return to your notes later to remind yourself of the passages you found particularly useful or thought-provoking.

Fourth, apply the advice given throughout *Morning Makeover*. For example, in *Part II*, I give you a 10-step plan for creating a quality morning routine that supports your goals. Don't just read about the 10 steps. Actually *do them*.

Fifth, periodically review your notes and revisit select passages. Why? Because you're going to forget a lot of what you read. That's true for everyone. By reviewing your notes and reprocessing your favorite sections, you'll commit them to memory. That's an important part of the learning process.

Sixth, share this information with someone you know. This is a highly-effective way to learn new material. The Roman philosopher Seneca said "When we teach, we learn." This is called the Protégé Effect.

If you do these six things, I'm confident *Morning Makeover* will have a dramatic impact on your life. But it's entirely up to you. As I've noted in my other books, you're the captain of your ship. You determine your destination and choose the path to reach it.

But if you're open to suggestions, I strongly recommend doing the six things outlined above.

With that out of the way, let's roll up our sleeves and dig into the good stuff. We're going to start by taking a close look at how sleep affects your ability to maintain a quality morning routine.

- Improve AM mood
- Not feel so stressed + rushed
- Be more patient, tolerant + kind w/kids
- Start day w/spiritual food
- Meditation
- Look better (do hair + makeup)
- eat healthy breakfast

PART I

HOW TO SET THE STAGE FOR A SUCCESSFUL MORNING

∾

Your ability to maintain your morning routine, day after day, will be influenced by the quality of your nighttime sleep. If you sleep well, you'll be more inclined to stick to your morning rituals. If you sleep poorly, you'll be tempted to hit the snooze button and remain under the covers. For this reason, it's important to plan your evenings to support quality slumber.

That's what we'll cover in *Part I* of *Morning Makeover*. We'll talk about the role of restful sleep as well as tactics that'll ensure you experience it night after night. We'll also address whether it's necessary to be an early riser, along with some of the reasons you might want to become one.

THE ROLE OF RESTFUL SLEEP

❧

I t's not enough to go to bed at a decent time (though that's important). The *quality* of your sleep matters. How many times have you gone to bed at a decent hour only to wake up in the morning feeling tired? That indicates you didn't go through all of your sleep stages (more on sleep stages in a moment).

The quality of your sleep affects how you feel the following day. It determines whether you feel motivated to get up. It influences your creativity. It impacts your productivity. Your sleep quality also affects your physical health.[1]

Restful sleep is crucial if you want to adopt a new habit, such as a purposeful morning routine. As I mentioned, if you fail to get sufficient rest at night, you'll be less inclined to perform your routine. Instead, you'll reach for the snooze button. When you finally drag yourself out of bed, you'll meander listlessly until you're forced to rush in order to get where you need to be.

I found this to be the case in my own life. I used to go to bed at midnight each night and get up at 4:00 a.m. each morning. I was able to get work done simply because I was up early and wired on coffee. But my productivity left a lot to be desired, as did the quality of my work.

I wasn't getting enough sleep. Coffee was the only thing keeping me going. But it's a poor substitute for a well-rested mind. Consequently, I'd mill about and waste time - time that would have been better spent sleeping.

Now I know better. I still get up early, but I go to bed earlier to make sure I get enough sleep.

How Sleep Stages Work (And Why They Matter)

The term "sleep quality" isn't well-defined. Researchers disagree regarding what actually constitutes good sleep.[2] But for practical purposes, we can make a few assumptions based on what we've learned about the brain.

We know that the brain goes through four sleep stages as we sleep. Following is a brief summary of these stages:

- **Stage 1**: light sleep that's easily interrupted.
- **Stage 2**: a deeper sleep stage.
- **Stage 3**: the deepest sleep stage. You're largely unaware of what is happening in your immediate environment.
- **Stage 4**: REM (rapid-eye-movement) sleep. The brain's activity is at its highest point during this stage. Dreams often occur.

(Note: sleep experts used to highlight five distinct stages of sleep. This practice ended in 2008 when stages 3 and 4 of the model used at the time were combined.)

Each cycle (stage 1 through stage 4) lasts between 90 and 120 minutes. The brain goes through multiple cycles each night, alternating between REM (rapid-eye-movement) sleep and NREM (non-rapid-eye-movement).

To feel completely rested, your brain must experience all four stages (a complete cycle) without interruption. Ideally, it would go through multiple cycles without interruption. Scientists have discovered that, in some ways, interrupted sleep may be worse than no sleep at all.[3]

REM sleep, in particular, is important because that's when your brain processes information and memories. It has a significant influence on your brain's performance during wakeful hours. If your sleep is routinely interrupted before your brain reaches REM sleep, you're likely to experience difficulty concentrating the following day.

I admit, the above information is a bit weighty. I prefer to focus on practical, actionable advice. But in my opinion, understanding how sleep stages work is critical to being able to maintain a quality morning routine. Everything begins with experiencing restful slumber, night after night. Once you understand how sleep stages work, you can take steps to ensure your brain enjoys the highest-quality, most restful sleep possible.

In the next section, I'll give you a number of helpful tips for improving the quality of your sleep.

[1]   https://www.nhlbi.nih.gov/health/health-topics/topics/sdd/why

[2] https://www.ncbi.nlm.nih.gov/pubmed/18929313

[3] http://www.hopkinsmedicine.org/news/media/releases/sleep-_interruptions_worse_for_mood_than_overall_reduced_amount_of_sleep_study_finds

10 QUICK TIPS TO ENSURE YOU GET A GOOD NIGHT'S SLEEP (EVERY NIGHT!)

~

I f you sleep well each night, and get up every morning feeling completely rested, you can skip this section. However, if you regularly wake up feeling tired, sluggish, or irritable, you'll benefit from the following tips. They'll help you to improve the quality of your sleep, which will have a positive influence on the rest of your day.

How will you benefit? You'll fall asleep faster (no more staring at the ceiling in frustration). You'll be more likely to enjoy uninterrupted rest (no more waking up multiple times throughout the night, disrupting your sleep cycles). And you'll wake up feeling refreshed and ready to start your day (no more dragging yourself out of bed, feeling as if you were hit by a train).

Put the following 10 tips to use, and I'm confident you'll wake up feeling more rested and energized.

#1 - Go To Bed At The Same Time Each Evening

Your body has an internal clock, often called its circadian rhythm. It's sometimes referred to as the body's sleep/wake cycle. It's the reason you feel tired at night and wakeful during the day.

This internal clock is most effective when you go to sleep at the same time each night. If your sleep patterns are irregular - you go to bed at different times throughout the week - this "clock" can't do its job. The result is that you might regularly experience difficulty getting to sleep.

Identify the time that you normally feel tired. Commit to going to bed at that time each evening.

#2 - Stop Consuming Caffeine Six Hours Before Bedtime

Caffeine is a stimulant. That's the reason millions of people drink coffee throughout the day. But it's important to realize that it can take hours for the effects of caffeine to wear off.

Give yourself six hours of caffeine-free time before going to bed. For example, if you normally go to bed at 10:00 p.m., stop consuming caffeine at 4:00 p.m.

Keep in mind, coffee isn't the only culprit. Caffeine can be found in chocolate and protein bars, as well as many sodas and teas. There's even a small amount in decaffeinated coffee.

#3 - Create An Environment Conducive To Sleeping

Are the lights in your bedroom glaringly bright? Do you have a large-display digital alarm clock near your bed? Is your mattress uncomfortable, making it difficult for you to fall asleep?

Your bedroom should be a refuge from everything that might otherwise keep you awake or disturb your slumber. The good news is that you're in control of its design. You get to determine the extent to which it supports your ability to sleep peacefully.

Here are a few ideas:

- Dim the lights
- Turn your alarm clock around so it faces away from you
- Invest in a comfortable mattress and pillow
- If you have a television in your bedroom, remove it
- If dry air causes you to experience respiratory problems, invest in a humidifier
- Use white noise to mask annoying sounds (dripping faucet, loud neighbors, etc.)
- If your dog is a restless sleeper, set up his bed outside your bedroom

#4 - Turn Off Electronic Devices An Hour Before Bedtime

We use our gadgets in a myriad of ways to improve our lives. For example, we connect with friends and loved ones through texts and emails. We look up recipes to plan meals for our families. We pay bills and manage our investments. We record our favorite television shows so that we can enjoy them at our leisure.

It's difficult to imagine life without our array of gadgets.

But these same gadgets can hamper your ability to sleep. If you're using your phone or tablet right before going to bed, don't be surprised if you feel completely awake when it's time to turn off the lights. Researchers have found that the blue light emitted by these devices can wreak havoc on your circadian rhythm.[1]

Set aside your devices at least one hour before bedtime.

#5 - Exercise Every Day

Exercise not only helps you to fall asleep at night, but also helps you to enjoy *better-quality* sleep. The more strenuous the activity, the greater the effect.

That doesn't mean you need to go to the gym and work up a sweat each day. Even a brisk 10-minute walk can do wonders. The key is to do it a few hours before bedtime, and do it consistently.

It may take a few weeks before you notice the difference in your sleep quality. But rest assured, the quality of your sleep *will* improve.

#6 - Avoid Sleeping In (Even On Weekends)

Remember the sleep/wake cycle, or circadian rhythm, I mentioned above? To make sure it works effectively, it's best to wake up at the same time each morning. Otherwise, you risk throwing your internal clock out of whack, which, in turn, will disrupt your ability to get to sleep at night.

It's tempting to sleep in, especially on the weekends and during the holidays. But while doing so may feel great in the moment, it can have a lasting negative impact on the quality of your sleep.

A better option is to wake up at your normal time each morning, and take a nap during the afternoon if you feel tired. It's less fun than sleeping in, but will pay dividends over the long run as your internal clock regulates itself.

Speaking of naps...

#7 - Limit The Duration Of Your Afternoon Naps

I love taking naps. There's nothing better than lying down on the couch, closing your eyes, and dozing off. You'll feel refreshed, more alert, and in a better mood. It's a great way to avoid the mid-afternoon slump, when your energy levels plummet.

But there's a right way and a wrong way to take naps. I've found that the best approach is to take them early in the afternoon (before 3:00 p.m.), and limit them to 20 minutes. If I take later naps, or nap for longer periods, it affects my ability to sleep at night.

#8 - Learn How To Use Light To Your Advantage

open blinds, turn lights on immediately

Your sleep/wake cycle is heavily influenced by a hormone called melatonin. This hormone, secreted by the brain, makes you feel sleepy. The amount secreted and released into the blood is influenced by the amount of light to which you're exposed. The more light there is in your immediate environment, the less melatonin your brain secretes.

This is the reason you feel awake when exposed to bright sunlight and drowsy in the evening, particularly when the lights are out.

Use this effect to your advantage. Avoid bright light before your bedtime. If outside light is entering through a window, put up curtains or shades to block it out. Also, as recommended above, avoid using your phone, tablet, and laptop, and watching television, right before going to bed. The light emitted by these devices can suppress melatonin secretion, making you feel less sleepy.

#9 - Avoid Drinking Two Hours Before Bedtime

The more you drink right before going to bed, the more likely you'll wake up and have to visit the bathroom. You may even have to make multiple visits.

Nighttime trips to the bathroom may seem harmless. But they can interrupt your sleep cycles, preventing you from enjoying undisturbed, deep sleep. That, of course, will affect how you feel in the morning.

Take your last sip of water at least two hours before you plan to go to sleep. That'll give you plenty of time to make one final bathroom trip before turning in for the evening.

#10 - Create And Follow An Evening Routine

There's no better way to guarantee you'll enjoy restful slumber at night than to follow a consistent nighttime routine.

Most of us are unable to go to sleep on demand. We have to ease our way into it. For example, I find that reading a novel helps to prepare my mind for bedtime. It relieves stress, relaxes me, and puts me in a good mood. You might find that taking a hot bath, listening to soft music, or practicing yoga has a similar effect on you.

Brainstorm a few activities that'll help you to wind down for the evening. Do them each night in the same order, starting at the same time. You'll find that the ritual will help you to shift from being awake to being ready to fall asleep within minutes of turning out the lights.

What If You're Still Unable To Sleep?

If you've acted on all 10 of the above suggestions, and you're still having difficulty getting to sleep, it's time to seek professional advice. Consult an expert licensed and board-certified in the treatment of sleep disorders.

Chronic sleeplessness is a serious issue. It can sap your energy, make you irritable, and impair your ability to focus. It can affect your memory and wreak havoc with your ability to make rational decisions. Long-standing insomnia can even lead to depression.

If your sleeplessness has persisted for more than a few weeks, seek the guidance of a specialist.

[1] http://www.health.harvard.edu/staying-healthy/blue-light-has-a-dark-side

MY EVENING ROUTINE (AND HOW IT HELPS ME TO SLEEP PEACEFULLY)

~

I thought it would be helpful to describe my evening routine, and explain the reasons behind its various components.

My routine is very simple. You can duplicate it with no effort. But it's worth underscoring that *your* nighttime routine should cater to *your* predilections.

For example, I choose not to perform yoga because I don't find it personally rewarding. If *you* enjoy yoga, and it helps you to relax, definitely consider making it a part of your evening ritual.

With that out of the way, here's how I spend the hours before climbing into bed.

- **5:00 p.m.** - Stop working. I think it's important to quit work at a reasonable hour. Quitting at 5:00 p.m. gives me plenty of time to relax.
- **5:15 p.m.** - Review the current day's to-do list and plan the next day.
- **6:00 p.m.** - Eat dinner. I rarely snack afterwards. I

sleep better when I eat several hours before going to bed.

- **6:30 p.m.** - Watch Netflix, "Ted" talks, or read a novel. These activities relax me.
- **8:00 p.m.** - Spend time with my wife.
- **10:00 p.m.** - Read a novel. Again, it's relaxing for me.
- **10:30 p.m.** - Take a hot shower, brush my teeth, and use the restroom. Nothing makes me sleepier than a hot shower.
- **11:00 p.m.** - Drink a glass of water. I realize this is inconsistent with the advice I offered in Tip #9 in the previous section. But I'm like a camel when it comes to drinking water. I'm unlikely to wake up in the middle of the night to visit the bathroom.
- **11:15 p.m.** - Fall asleep.

Notice how most of the activities above are designed for relaxation. But most importantly, note that I go through the same routine, night after night. Doing so conditions my brain. It signals that bedtime is coming. By the time I drink a glass of water at 11:00 p.m., I'm ready to fall asleep, and often do so the moment my head hits my pillow.

You don't have to follow my evening routine. In fact, you may dislike some of my favorite nighttime activities, such as reading novels. That's okay! Use my routine as an example, and design one that works for *you*.

If you enjoy meditating at night, make that a part of your routine. If you like practicing yoga or listening to soft music, include those activities. If you enjoy playing video games, do that (but stop an hour before bedtime).

The important point is that you create an evening ritual composed of activities that relax you and prepare you for sleep. Then, repeat it every night, preferably starting at the same time each night.

In the next section, we'll explore whether you need to be an early riser to get the most out of your mornings. The details may surprise you.

Kids

- pack tomorrow's lunches
- tidy house
- set out kid's clothes
- wash face, take pills
- read
- Netfix
- meditate
- tea
- 10pm SLEEP
- set out breakfast dishes

No kids

- gym
- meeting
- 2nd job
- 12am SLEEP

IS IT NECESSARY TO WAKE UP AT 5:00 A.M.?

~

You've probably heard that early risers are more productive than people who wake up later in the morning. It's a common assumption that getting up early is the key to enjoying explosive productivity. But does being an early riser truly make you more productive?

It's an intriguing idea: all you have to do is get up at 5:00 a.m., and you'll see a major increase in the volume of work you get done.

But scientists claim the connection is one of correlation, not causation. While early risers are often productive, it's not because they wake up early. They're productive due to other factors.

Several years ago, researchers in Switzerland and Belgium tracked the brain activity of 16 early risers and 15 late risers. These subjects got the same amount of sleep each night (seven hours), but the former got out of bed four hours earlier than the latter. The researchers found there was little difference in performance between the two groups on a series of tasks.[1]

Given these findings, why do so many productivity experts recommend getting up early? I think I've figured out the reason. Early risers tend to act with intention, an idea we explored in the section *The Importance Of Intentionality*. The problem is, the experts seldom mention this when they advise becoming an early riser.

When you *decide* to get up early, you do so with a purpose in mind. There's a reason you want to get an early start. This reason drives you, prompting you to take action. It's why you're more productive when you wake up early.

I'll use an example from my own life. As I mentioned, I used to wake up at 4:00 a.m. years ago. I did so to create websites and write. These were my intentions. Both were clearly defined in my mind as I climbed into bed each evening.

Because I had a purpose, I knew precisely what I was supposed to be doing each morning. Moreover, because I understood my reason for doing the two activities (to build a business), I woke up excited to get started. As a result, my productivity soared. I was able to complete a significant volume of work in the first three hours of my day.

(This was after I stopped going to bed at midnight each night. I started going to bed earlier to make certain I received enough sleep to perform well the following day.)

The point is, my productivity wasn't due to simply getting up early. It was due to having a clearly-defined *intention*. A purpose.

So is it necessary to start your morning routine at 5:00 a.m.? In my opinion, no. It's far more important that you wake up with intentionality, ready to take deliberate action. That, I believe, is the key to experiencing a truly productive and meaningful day.

Having said that, I confess that I'm a strong advocate of waking up early (I get up at 5:30 a.m. these days). It's not an overstatement to say that becoming an early riser changed my life. In the next section, I'll explain the main reasons.

[1]   http://www.rodalewellness.com/health/sleeping-late-and-productivity

10 REASONS TO WAKE UP EARLY

∼

I've always equated being an early riser with being productive. Of course, as noted in the previous section, getting up at the crack of dawn alone doesn't guarantee anything. The key to high productivity in the morning is waking up with a specific purpose in mind.

Having said that, there are numerous advantages to getting up early that extend beyond the volume of work you can complete while everyone else is sleeping. Set your alarm an hour early, and avoid hitting the snooze button, and here are some of the rewards you'll experience.

#1 - You'll Enjoy Peace And Quiet

One of the great joys of waking up early is that few others do so. That means there's less noise to distract you. Whether you arrive at your workplace before anyone else or relax at home before your family wakens, you'll savor the peace and quiet.

There are fewer cars on the road; fewer people on the streets; and fewer phone calls, emails, texts to address.

#2 - You'll Be More Creative

It's not that dragging yourself out of bed early makes you more creative. It doesn't. But many people find they're more creative in the morning than they are in the afternoon or evening.

This might stem from the fact that the mind is fresh and well-rested. It might also be due to the peace and quiet that accompany the early-morning hours.

It's worth noting that some studies show that night owls actually experience more creative breakthroughs than early risers. The problem is, staying up through the early-morning hours isn't conducive to a normal work schedule. Most people find it's far more effective to get a great night's sleep and wake up early and fully rested the next morning.

#3 - You'll Feel More Proactive

In 2009, Harvard biologist Christoph Randler reported an interesting finding after surveying 367 college students. He noted that students who woke up early were more likely to feel more proactive. Randler opined that this attribute led to higher income and better job performance.

Is the act of getting up early directly responsible for increasing one's proactivity? Not according to Randler. He points to studies that suggest being an early riser makes one more *conscientious*. This conscientiousness, he claims, is the true reason early risers tend to be more proactive.

#4 - You'll Experience Less Stress

Decreased stress for early risers stems from two factors. First, they have more time in the morning. This extra time allows them to address the things they need to get done without feeling rushed.

Second, they're less burdened with mental clutter. Such clutter accumulates throughout the day as we address to-do items and interact with people. It's all but nonexistent in the early-morning hours.

As we'll discuss later, you'll also find that performing your morning ritual will help keep your stress levels in check.

#5 - You'll Feel More In Control

Think back to the last time you felt harried in the morning. Maybe you were under pressure to get your children ready for school on time. Perhaps you were forced to skip breakfast to attend an 8:00 a.m. meeting at your workplace. Maybe you had to dispense with showering so you'd have enough time to show up at an important early-morning doctor's appointment.

Whatever the circumstances, you probably felt as if you lacked control of your morning.

When you get up early, these challenges disappear. You have more time at your disposal, and thus more freedom to get important things done in preparation for the rest of your day.

#6 - You'll Have More Time To Exercise

Have you ever planned to exercise in the late afternoon, perhaps after returning home from your job, only to end up on the couch watching television? This is a common scenario. It results from low willpower which, in turn, stems from decision fatigue.

Here's how the process works:

You make hundreds of decisions throughout the day. Each one whittles away at your willpower. By the time you arrive at home, the idea of watching television is more appealing than going to the gym. You surrender to its siren call, promising yourself you'll visit the gym tomorrow.

You can easily short-circuit this pattern by waking up early and exercising in the morning. You'll have plenty of time to exercise so it's unlikely you'll cancel. Plus, you won't have to depend on a waning reserve of willpower for motivation.

#7 - You'll Be Less Likely To Procrastinate

All of us have a tendency to procrastinate. It's human nature, particularly when it involves activities we find unappealing.

This tendency stems from the way we decide between conflicting options. According to Timothy A. Pychyl, author of *Solving The Procrastination Puzzle*, every decision is a battle waged between the prefrontal cortex and limbic system. The prefrontal cortex is in charge of making (hopefully good) decisions. Meanwhile, the limbic system tries to pursue the activity that promises the most gratification. At the end of the day, when our willpower is at its lowest point, we're more likely to give in to the appeals of our limbic system.

How does being an early riser solve this problem? When you get up early, there are fewer activities vying for your attention. You have fewer options. As a result, you'll be more inclined to tackle whatever you need to get done.

#8 - You'll Avoid Having To Rush

Early risers have plenty of time to get ready in the morning. They can relax as they glide through their morning routines, confident they'll reach their destination (e.g. the office, school, an early dental appointment, etc.) on time.

By contrast, late risers tend to feel rushed in the morning. They scramble to get showered and dressed, and often skip breakfast to get out the door on time.

Speaking of breakfast...

#9 - You'll Have Time For (A Real) Breakfast

Pop-Tarts are not a real breakfast. Neither are protein bars, frozen waffles, or muffins. Even most breakfast cereals, which may seem nutritious on the surface, are little more than highly-processed sugar bombs.

People consume these "foods" because they're fast and convenient. I used to do it, too. Waking up late, I didn't have time to fix a real breakfast. So I'd devour this type of junk, wash it down with coffee, and head out the door.

When you become an early riser, you can take the time to eat healthy food. For example, scramble a few eggs (assuming you don't have an egg allergy), enjoy some oatmeal, and eat some fruit. You'll feel better and have more energy. You'll also avoid the mid-morning crash that typically follows a high-sugar breakfast.

#10 - You'll Get More Work Done

At 5:00 a.m., the house is quiet. Everyone is still asleep, giving you the tranquility you need to focus on your work (after completing your morning routine, of course).

That work might entail writing a blog post, writing in a journal, or penning your first novel. Or maybe you need to put the finishing touches on an important presentation for your job. Whatever type of work you need to complete, the quietude of the early morning hours is a boon for those who need to get things done.

That's Merely The Tip Of The Iceberg

There are many other reasons to wake up early, of course. For example, I've found that doing so makes me more disciplined. It also improves my attitude and disposition.

Having said that, if you're like me, the 10 advantages described above are the ones that are likely to have the biggest impact on your day.

[1] http://onlinelibrary.wiley.com/doi/10.1111/j.1559-1816.2009.00549.x/abstract

HOW TO WAKE UP FEELING INVIGORATED

~

W aking up early, by itself, isn't enough to guarantee a successful day, or even a successful morning. You need to wake up *with energy*. That's the difference between looking spitefully at your alarm clock through half-opened, groggy eyes and leaving your bed feeling refreshed and invigorated.

A good night's sleep does wonders, of course. But there are many other things you can do to ensure you feel energetic when your alarm clock sounds.

Here are a few quick ideas I've found helpful in my own life:

Set Your Alarm To Play Sounds You Enjoy

Most alarm clocks make a jarring, abrasive sound when they go off. They're designed that way. The problem is, if the first sound you hear in the morning makes you want to break something, you won't be in a positive frame of mind. And that makes it difficult to get out of bed feeling excited and full of energy.

Don't consign yourself to waking up to an obnoxious alarm clock. Program your phone to play your favorite song. Or program it to emit a soft, pleasant ringtone.

I've programmed the alarm on my phone to emit a gentle, futuristic tone that rises in note until I turn it off. I find it inspiring. It helps me to start my morning on the right foot.

Clear Your Head

If you've had a busy or stressful day, your head is going to be filled with thoughts and worries, even after you set aside your work. That's natural. The problem is, if you go to bed in such a state, you'll have difficulty falling asleep. Worse, when you finally manage to get to sleep, the runaway thoughts and worries can make your slumber fitful.

Spend 10 minutes before bedtime clearing your head. I recommend practicing mindful meditation because it works for me. It's easy. Sit, close your eyes, and focus on your breathing. You'll find that doing so not only has a calming effect, but will also clear your mind of rampant thoughts.

Find A Balance Between Too Hot And Too Cold

On cold nights, it's tempting to sleep under an extra-heavy blanket. On hot nights, it's tempting to open the windows and point a couple fans at your bed, or sleep with the air conditioner running.

The goal, of course, is to be comfortable while you sleep. But it's easy to make yourself too hot or too cold. And *that* can negatively affect the quality of your sleep.[1]

Note the ambient temperature of your bedroom in the evening. Then, avoid going to extremes to counter too-high or too-low temps. Instead of crawling under a extra-heavy blanket, consider using a lighter one. Instead of turning on your home's

A/C while you sleep, consider setting up a fan that oscillates rather than points directly at your bed.

The goal is to maintain a consistent body temperature while you sleep. If you manage to do so, you'll feel more energetic when you wake up in the morning.

Wake Up To Light

Waking up early is difficult enough, especially when you first adopt the habit. Trying to do it in darkness makes it even more difficult. Waking up early is easier when you do it to light.

Ideally, you'd wake up to natural sunlight. I've found that natural light has an energizing effect on me.

Having said that, the direction your windows face and the time you get up in the morning may preclude natural sunlight as an option. For example, if your bedroom windows face west, the sun won't do you much good. Likewise if you intend to wake up before sunrise.

Fortunately, you have other options. For example, you can buy a timer that turns on your bedroom lights at a preselected time. Or you can buy a wake-up light alarm clock. The point is that waking up to light can make you feel more energetic.

Get Out Of Bed Immediately

Every moment you spend in bed after turning off your alarm clock (or phone) increases the likelihood that you'll go back to sleep. That's natural. It's dark. It's early. The mind is still trying to clear the cobwebs that accompany waking up. Going back to sleep is the path of least resistance.

Short-circuit that natural response by getting out of bed the moment you wake up.

That may present a challenge if you're accustomed to hitting the snooze button. If that's the case, try positioning your clock or phone far enough away from your bed that you're forced to get *out* of bed to turn it off.

Get A Sufficient Amount Of Sleep

This is probably intuitive. But it's worth emphasizing the point.

The best way to feel energized in the morning is to make sure you get a good night's sleep. That means going to bed at a reasonable hour. It also means sticking to a predictable evening routine so your brain learns when it's time to go to sleep.

Keep in mind, a single night of good sleep may not suffice. If you fail to get sufficient sleep night after night, you'll accumulate a sleep debt[2], setting the stage for mental and physical fatigue. Worse, the greater this debt, the longer it'll take to "pay off."

Once your sleep debt is finally paid off, you'll find it easier to wake up feeling energetic.

Review Your Purpose

This isn't scientific. I just know that it works for me. I suspect it'll work for you, too.

We discussed the reasons it's vital to have a purpose when creating and following a morning routine in the section *The Importance Of Intentionality*. I've found that reviewing my purpose immediately after waking fills me with energy. It gets me excited to get the day started. I know precisely why I'm getting up. And aided by my to-do list, I know the activities I need to address to accomplish the day's goals.

Give it a try. Review your intentions, or purpose, when you wake up. Think about what you hope to accomplish that day as you perform your morning routine. Assuming your goals excite you, you're almost certain to feel invigorated.

Again, it works for me. I'm confident you'll have the same experience.

Coming Up Next...

We've just laid the groundwork for developing a quality morning routine that'll help to ensure you experience a successful day. In *Part II*, we'll go through the step-by-step process of creating a routine that works for you.

[1] https://www.ncbi.nlm.nih.gov/pubmed/18192289

[2]   https://www.scientificamerican.com/article/fact-or-fiction-can-you-catch-up-on-sleep/

PART II

10 STEPS TO CREATING A PERFECT MORNING ROUTINE

∽

There's no single correct morning routine. As mentioned earlier, the key is to come up with a series of activities that support your intentions and become habit.

If your intention is to lose weight, going for an early-morning jog and eating a high-protein breakfast may be ideal. If your intention is to find your center before heading into a chaotic workplace, breathing exercises and mindful meditation may be the ticket.

In this section of *Morning Makeover*, we're going to create the perfect morning routine for *you*. We'll go through the careful process, step by step, of designing a routine that delivers the physical and cognitive benefits you desire.

The 10 steps that follow require a bit of self-analysis and reflection. But the effort is worthwhile. These 10 steps are integral to enjoying the rewards that accompany a quality morning ritual.

STEP 1: IDENTIFY YOUR "WHY"

"If you have a strong purpose in life, you don't have to be pushed. Your passion will drive you there." - Roy T. Bennett, author of *The Light in the Heart*

HAVING a strong purpose makes your effort meaningful. That's crucial. It can make the difference between sticking to your routine each morning and choosing to hit the snooze button. You're more likely to maintain a new habit if your reasons for doing so are important to you.

For example, suppose your goal is to feel more relaxed in the morning. Your workplace is stressful, and it's vital that you arrive there in a calm frame of mind. You've defined your goal and have a general sense of your reasons for pursuing it. But you haven't yet clearly defined the latter. If you neglect to do so, you'll be less compelled to follow through on whatever morning activities you've chosen to make you feel more relaxed.

Ask yourself: *why* is it important that you arrive at work in a calm state of mind? Following are a few possibilities. When you're calm...

- You're more efficient.
- You're more productive.
- You're able to make better decisions.
- You're in a better mood when you come home.
- You're able to enjoy your work rather than dread it.

If any of the above reasons resonate with you, they comprise your "why." Being aware of these reasons gives you motivation. They'll prompt you to rise in the morning and perform the activities you've chosen rather than automatically reaching for the snooze button.

Here's What To Do Right Now

Sit down with a pen and pad of paper. Brainstorm daily goals that are important to you. Here are a few examples:

- Feel more relaxed
- Be more productive
- Feel healthier
- Look better
- Show up at work on time
- Get your kids ready for school without rushing
- Maintain a cheery disposition
- Keep your workstation free of clutter
- Have more time to spend with friends
- Avoid unnecessary conflict at home

The above is merely scratching the surface, of course. The important point is that you identify the daily goals *you* want to achieve. These will be the reasons that compel you to wake up and perform your morning routine each day.

Why?

- Better attitude/mood
- No rushing
- Patient w/kids
- Look better (hair/makeup done)
- Be on time!
- Guarantee daily med
- Daily exercise
- Better breakfast

STEP 2: MAKE A LIST OF POTENTIAL
OBSTACLES

~

I
f you've grown accustomed to hitting the snooze button and
then scrambling to get out the door each morning,
adopting a morning routine won't be easy. You're going to
face internal resistance. Your mind and body will conspire to
keep you in bed where it's warm and comfortable. When you
finally drag yourself out of bed, they'll encourage you to check
your phone for texts, watch the news, or play video games.

In other words, you're going to face potential stumbling
blocks as you ritualize your mornings.

The motivations for staying in bed, sleeping in, and wasting
your mornings can be traced back to any number of causes. It's
important to identify these causes so you can take steps to
avoid them.

For example, many people fail to stick to their morning
routines because they feel exhausted when their alarm clocks go
off. This exhaustion creates enormous internal resistance. It's
more compelling to stay in bed than to get up and perform a
morning routine.

In this scenario, willpower isn't the answer. You may be able to will yourself out of bed once or twice, but it's a poor long-term solution. Plus, it won't do you any good to drag yourself out of bed when you feel exhausted.

Rather, to overcome this particular obstacle, it's important to identify its underlying causes. Are you getting enough sleep? Are you going to bed at the same time each night? Are you doing something that interrupts your sleep, preventing you from enjoying complete, 4-stage sleep cycles? An example would be drinking a lot of water right before bed, precipitating a need to visit the bathroom in the middle of the night.

Once you've identified the factors that are producing a given obstacle, you can make adjustments to resolve it. In our example, that might entail the following:

- Going to bed an hour earlier
- Going to bed at 10:00 p.m. each night
- Avoiding drinking more than a few ounces of water an hour before bedtime

Use this process to resolve any obstacle that's making it difficult for you to wake up and perform your morning ritual. Identify the stumbling block, and identify the causal factors.

For example, if you habitually hit the snooze button, your alarm clock may be too close to your bed, making doing so an irresistible temptation.

If you lack motivation to start your day, you may have neglected to properly define your intentions.

If you sleep poorly at night, the issue might be related to using your phone, iPad, and other gadgets right before bedtime.

Once you've identified the *reasons* you struggle to start your mornings on the right foot, resolving them should become a relatively simple matter.

Here's What To Do Right Now

Make a list of negative feelings, both mental and physical, that you experience in the morning. Here are a few examples:

- Do you feel exhausted when you wake up?
- Do you feel unmotivated?
- Do you dread getting out of bed and starting your day? *yes!*
- Do you feel stressed out?
- Do you experience physical pain?

These things sabotage your mornings. But you don't have to be a victim to them. Once you identify your personal stumbling blocks, you can investigate their primary causes. That'll reveal what actions you need to take to short-circuit their effects and overcome them.

- Move phone/alarm across room
- Get light timer
- Buy books
- Auto coffee maker

STEP 3: DETERMINE HOW MUCH TIME
YOU NEED

~

Most of us have a limited amount of time in the morning before we have to be somewhere or meet a specific obligation. For example, we might have to drop our kids off at school by 8:15 a.m. Or we have to get to the office by 8:30 a.m.

Most people believe they know how much time they need to get ready in the morning. The problem is, their assumptions are often vague, and even inaccurate. That can wreak havoc on your efforts to incorporate a quality morning routine.

So let's work backwards. Identify your day's first obligation. Think about everything that needs to happen from the moment you wake up until you meet that obligation. Then, consider how much time each activity requires.

Let's use getting to the office by 8:30 a.m. as an example. Here's how the breakdown of activities might appear (again, working backwards).

- 5 minutes - walk from your workplace parking lot to your office
- 40 minutes - commute from home to your workplace
- 5 minutes - say goodbye to your spouse and kids
- 20 minutes - prepare and eat breakfast
- 10 minutes - get dressed
- 30 minutes - shower and fix hair
- 5 minutes - apply makeup (for the ladies)
- 10 minutes - wake up, wash face, brush teeth, and use the bathroom

The above process requires 2 hours and 5 minutes. That's the minimum amount of time you'll need to complete it. So if you intend to be at your office at 8:30 a.m., you'd need to set your alarm no later than 6:25 a.m.

If you like to plan conservatively, you might set it 15 minutes earlier to allow for unanticipated traffic accidents during your commute and other snafus. Doing so would entail waking up at 6:10 a.m.

This is useful information.

Suppose your *new* morning routine - the one that precedes the process outlined above - requires 45 minutes. If that's the case, you'll need to wake up at 5:25 a.m. That'll give you the time you need to get to your office by 8:30 a.m. If your new routine only requires 15 minutes, you'll need to wake up at 5:55 a.m.

In subsequent steps, we'll specify how much time each activity in your morning routine will take. This step will guarantee you'll have enough time to perform all of them.

Here's What To Do Right Now

First, write down everything that needs to happen between the time you wake up and the time you have to meet the day's first obligation.

Second, estimate the number of minutes each activity requires. Be conservative where appropriate - for example, your morning commute.

Third, determine the absolute latest you can wake up in the morning and still meet your obligation. Skipping important activities, such as showering or eating breakfast, is not an option.

We now have a baseline. As we create your morning routine in the following steps, it'll become clearer when you'll actually need to wake up.

STEP 4: SELECT HABITS THAT ALIGN WITH YOUR INTENTIONS

∼

W e talked about the role of intentions in creating and maintaining your morning routine in the section *The Importance Of Intentionality*. And in *Step 1: Identify Your "Why,"* you spent time brainstorming daily goals that are meaningful to you. That prepared us for this step: choosing morning activities that support your intentions.

It's simple to do. You know intuitively which habits are likely to be helpful. It's just a matter of creating a morning routine that includes them. This step formalizes that process.

For example, suppose you'd like to feel more energetic. Here are a few activities that'll help you realize that goal:

- Go for a morning jog
- Eat a high-protein breakfast
- Drink a glass of ice-cold water
- Practice yoga
- Take a cold shower

Or suppose you'd like to have a sunnier disposition. You might choose to do the following each morning:

- Read a chapter from an inspiring book
- Listen to an uplifting podcast
- Write a short love note to your spouse
- Create a list of things for which you're thankful
- Tell a family member how much you appreciate them

Suppose you want to feel more relaxed and in control of your day. The following habits can help:

- Make your bed when you wake up
- Practice mindful meditation
- Perform breathing exercises
- Write in a personal journal
- Visualize your day progressing perfectly

Or suppose you'd like to increase your daily productivity. Consider adding these habits to your morning routine:

- Review your day's to-do list
- Check in with an accountability partner
- Write down one outcome you must effect today
- Do some type of cardiovascular exercise
- Arrive at the office one hour before everyone else

The above are merely examples. Your morning routine is going to be unique to your circumstances and intentions. The important thing is that you select activities that support the goals you want to achieve.

Here's What To Do Right Now

In Step 1, you identified your "why," the reason you want to implement a morning routine. Now, create a list of activities that align with that purpose.

For example, if you'd like to feel less rushed in the morning, wake up 30 minutes earlier to give yourself more time to get ready. If you want to feel healthier, eat a nutritious breakfast that stabilizes your blood sugar levels. If you want to improve your focus, declutter your mind by writing down all of the thoughts swimming around in your head.

Next, create a list of habits that are inconsistent with your intention. These are the activities you want to *stop* doing in the morning. For example, if you want to feel less rushed, avoid watching the news and visiting social media. If you want to feel healthier, avoid high-sugar snacks. If you want to enjoy better focus, avoid checking your phone for new texts every few minutes.

Knowing which habits to cut is just as important as knowing which ones to include in your morning routine.

- Reading Daily Reflections, Bible, B. Book
- Prayer
- Inventory
- Meditation
- Journalling
- Gratitude list
- Uplifting text to friends
- Healthy breakfast
- Exercise

Inconsistent
- snooze button
- phone
- TV
- unplanned projects

STEP 5: CHOOSE ACTIVITIES THAT MAXIMIZE YOUR ENERGY

~

Doing things that increase your energy in the morning is helpful regardless of what your main intentions are. For example, my morning routines are designed to boost my productivity. That's my primary purpose for getting up early and performing the activities I've included in my routines.

But I know high energy levels are crucial if I want to remain productive throughout the day. So some of my chosen activities are included for that purpose.

For example, here's a routine I use to increase my writing productivity:

- **5:25 a.m.** - Wake up.
- **5:30 a.m.** - Splash cold water on my face, brush my teeth, get my hair under control, and use the restroom.
- **5:40 a.m.** - Drink 8 oz. of cold water.
- **5:45 a.m.** - Do stretching exercises.
- **5:50 a.m.** - Pray and meditate.

- **5:55 a.m.** - Commit to completing a certain volume of writing for the day.
- **6:00 a.m.** - Leave for Starbucks.
- **6:10 a.m.** - Drink a Caffè Americano while reading material from my favorite non-fiction authors.
- **6:40 a.m.** - Write while listening to Mozart's Alla Turca or Chopin's Prelude in E minor, Op 28 No. 4.
- **9:00 a.m.** - Return home and exercise (pushups).
- **9:15 a.m.** - Prepare and eat breakfast (a delicious steak).
- **9:45 a.m.** - Resume writing.

Notice that some of the activities, such as stretching and drinking a glass of cold water, don't directly influence my writing volume. But they *do* increase my energy. That, in turn, increases my writing productivity.

Think of activities that make *you* feel more energetic. Some folks feel energized after taking a brisk walk outside immediately upon waking. Others enjoy listening to uplifting music. Still others swear by taking cold showers.

It's a personal choice. Activities that work for others may not work for you. For example, I can't imagine taking a cold shower. But it works perfectly for a friend of mine.

The point is that activities that energize you should be a part of your morning routine even if "more energy" isn't your main intention. They can provide the fuel you need to effect the outcome you desire.

Here's What To Do Right Now

Write down a list of activities that energize you. Make your list comprehensive. Don't worry. You're not going to include all of these activities in your morning routine. But it's useful to have a complete list handy from which to choose the ones you *do* decide to include.

Organize your list using two columns. Write down an activity in the first column. Write down how it makes you feel in the second column. For example, splashing cold water on my face jolts me awake. Stretching loosens my joints and makes my body feel better. Drinking coffee makes me feel more creative.

Next, identify activities that sap your energy. Write them down on your list. Note how they make you feel.

For me, reading online forums makes me feel lethargic. Perusing news headlines makes me feel dispirited. Eating sugary foods derails my momentum as my blood sugar levels crash. I avoid doing these things in the morning because they have a negative effect on my productivity throughout the day.

Once you have a list of activities that increase your energy and a list of those that sap it, you're ready to create a quality morning routine. Onward to Step 6!

Increase Energy

- shower
- coffee
- 7min workout or jog/gym
- glass of water
- meditation
- inventory

Decrease Energy

- phone
- unplanned projects
- sugar
- TV

STEP 6: START WITH A SIMPLE PLAN

∾

T he first morning routine I created for myself was a complete bust. I wanted to make huge, *radical* changes to the way in which I spent my mornings. I adopted a take-no-prisoners attitude, unwilling to even consider the possibility of failure.

The result? Predictably, I failed.

Within days, I was back to my old shenanigans. I stayed in bed long after my alarm sounded; I ate unhealthy foods for breakfast; and I wasted a ton of time reading blogs, forums, and news websites.

Why did this happen? Why did I fail in adopting my morning routine in the beginning?

I'm convinced the answer is simple. I failed because I tried to change too many things at once. That was a recipe for failure for two reasons. First, old habits are hard to break. Second, new habits take time to become ingrained. Trying to break every bad habit while trying to adopt a long list of new habits was guaranteed to fail.

I didn't realize the causal effect immediately. I figured my failure was a matter of willpower. So, like a stubborn mule, I tried again and again, using the same take-no-prisoners approach.

The result? Failure. Again and again.

I eventually realized what was happening, and adopted the opposite approach. I restructured my morning by changing one habit at a time. During the first week, I focused on getting up earlier. The following week, I focused on drinking 8 oz. of cold water each morning. Next, I focused on doing stretching exercises for five minutes immediately after getting out of bed.

I used the same process to break my bad habits. Rather than trying to break all of them at once, I focused on overcoming them one at a time.

I often did this concurrently with the adoption of a *good* habit, especially if the two were related. For example, while training myself to wake up earlier, I also weaned myself from hitting the snooze button. While adopting the habit to read material from my favorite non-fiction authors, I weaned myself from reading useless blogs, forums, and news sites.

I found it was easier to *replace* bad habits rather than simply break them.

I recommend that you use this same approach when you implement your new morning routine. Start with a simple plan and add to it gradually. Although it'll take more time to put your entire routine into action, you'll have more success in making it stick.

Here's What To Do Right Now

In Step 4, we created a list of activities that support your intentions. We also created a list of activities that work against them. Review those two lists and look for opportunities to replace bad habits with good ones.

For example, suppose your intention is to lose weight. Your

list of supportive activities might include "eat a nutritious break-fast." Your list of non-supportive activities might include "avoid pastries." The former can replace the latter. Take these opportunities to replace bad habits with good ones.

Next, create a simple morning routine that includes five easy activities. If you want to lose weight, these might include weighing yourself, drinking a glass of cold water, and taking vitamins. It's crucial that these five "starter" activities are easy to perform. That'll help you to overcome any resistance posed by your mind.

Spend the first week focusing only on these five activities. Because they're easy to perform and can be done so within the space of a few minutes, it's okay to lump them together. The important thing is that they'll form the foundation on which we'll add more difficult habits later.

STEP 7: STREAMLINE YOUR MORNING ROUTINE

~

New habits always trigger internal resistance. The reason is because our brains are wired to do what we've done in the past. It loves routine.

On the one hand, that's good. Once you've performed your morning routine, day after day, for months, your brain will prompt you to do so each morning. Your routine will become automatic.

On the other hand, this same trait makes it difficult to change your *current* routine. Your brain is accustomed to your current habits. If you normally watch television right after getting out of bed, you'll experience resistance when you replace that habit with a new one, such as jogging, yoga, or meditation.

The key is to minimize this resistance.

Adopting (or replacing) one major habit at a time, as we discussed in Step 6, helps. But we can go further. We can reduce resistance even more by streamlining our morning activities. And we do *that* by preparing the night before.

For example, let's suppose you want to replace watching television with jogging. That's a major change, and you're almost certain to face internal resistance to it. How can you minimize that resistance, making it as easy as possible to get out the door for a morning jog? Here are a few things you can do the night before:

- Position your running shoes at the side of your bed.
- Fill a glass with cold water and place it on your nightstand (hydration is important if you plan to exert yourself).
- Choose the route you'll jog.
- Sleep in the clothes you'll wear during your jog.
- Go to bed early enough to get sufficient sleep.

Doing these things removes small obstacles that stand in your way. For example, it'll be easier to overcome resistance if you don't have to search for your running shoes in the morning. Likewise, sleeping in your running clothes removes a preparatory step that might otherwise distract and dissuade you from going for an early-morning jog.

Use this process to lessen the resistance you'll face with every major change you make to your current morning routine. The more you streamline your new routine, the greater success you'll have in actually sticking to it.

Here's What To Do Right Now

Review your list of new activities that support your intentions (again, we created this list in Step 4). Consider each one and come up with ways to streamline it.

For example, suppose you intend to eat a nutritious breakfast consisting of eggs and bacon. Do the following the night before:

- Set a frying pan on the stove

- Place a plate and silverware on the kitchen table
- Place a glass of water on the kitchen table
- Remove three eggs from the carton
- Remove three slices of bacon from the package and put them in a Ziploc bag

When you walk into your kitchen in the morning, several preparatory steps will have already been handled. As a result, you'll face fewer obstacles and less resistance to eating a nutritious breakfast.

Go through this process for each new activity on your list. Brainstorm ways to save time and effort. No effort is too small to consider as even small savings can have a significant cumulative effect.

- H₂O at bedside
- Breakfast items set out
- Coffee set up
- Kid's clothes pre-picked out
- Lunches made
- Reading materials on counter

STEP 8: FAMILIARIZE YOURSELF WITH "HABIT STACKING"

~

One of the keys to establishing any new habit is to have a reliable trigger. A trigger is an event that prompts you to take a particular action. It stimulates an automatic urge to act in a given way. If the trigger is deep-rooted, you end up taking action without thinking about doing so. The action becomes an automatic response to the trigger.

For example, I splash cold water on my face immediately after waking up. Getting out of bed in the morning serves as the trigger. I don't have to *think* about dousing my face with cold water. I simply *do* it, like Pavlov's dogs salivating at the sound of the dinner bell.

Triggers are critical to forming habit stacks. A habit stack is a series of activities that occur in a predefined sequence. Each activity in the sequence serves as the trigger for the activity following it.

For example, consider the following sequence of morning events:

- Wake up
- Turn alarm clock off
- Get out of bed
- Brush teeth
- Use restroom
- Take shower
- Blow-dry hair
- Apply makeup
- Get dressed

This sequence is a habit stack. The individual activities are executed in the same order each morning. Importantly, each activity triggers the one following it.

Habit stacks are useful because they encourage us to complete our morning routines without having to think about the individual habits that comprise them. Once we perform the first activity in the stack, our routines develop their own momentum.

To fully appreciate how this works, remember that a habit stack is comprised of more than just a series of random activities; it's comprised of a series of *triggers*.

Here's What To Do Right Now

Review the list of activities you created in Step 4. Play around with their order.

Some will logically follow others. For example, if you want to start jogging in the morning, you'll want to shower *afterwards*. If writing in a journal is a part of your desired routine, you might find it helpful to start with a cup of coffee.

Arrange the activities you want to pursue into a workable stack. Start with strong habits you've already adopted, and build upon them. Your brain is already accustomed to performing these activities. By attaching new habits to deeply-rooted ones, your brain can streamline the habit adoption process.

For example, you (hopefully) brush your teeth each morning. It's an ingrained part of your routine. If you'd like to start writing in a journal, do it immediately after you brush your teeth. Use the deeply-rooted habit (brushing your teeth) to expedite the adoption of the new habit (journal writing).

Don't just string together multiple new habits and activities, and expect them to take root. Together, they'll generate too much resistance. Instead, pair new ones with old ones to form mini-stacks. Then, combine the mini-stacks together to form a larger stack.

I think you'll find it's the quickest way to create a morning routine that's easy to perform with consistency.

STEP 9: WRITE DOWN YOUR MORNING ROUTINE

~

Step 9 is the simplest of the lot. But don't underestimate its importance.

I'm an advocate of writing down your morning routine using pen and paper. Don't trust your memory. Don't put it in the cloud using Evernote or OneNote. Don't put it into a Microsoft Word document.

Write it down on paper.

I recommend doing this for three reasons. First, writing focuses your mind on the item being written. Research shows that writing requires a different cognitive process than typing.[1] This process engages the brain in a unique way that leads to better comprehension and improved retention.

Second, writing down your morning routine eliminates the need to memorize it. I learned years ago that I couldn't trust my memory. If I didn't write things down, there was a good chance I'd forget about them. If you face the same challenge - frankly, I suspect most people do - you can easily solve it by writing down your routine.

Third, writing things down makes your intentions feel more salient. If you're like me, it'll make you feel more committed to achieving them. When you wake up and see your morning routine on paper, you'll feel more inclined to perform it.

Here's What To Do Right Now

Review the morning routine (or habit stack) you created in Step 8.

Next, take a piece of paper and divide it into two columns. Write down each activity in your routine in the left column. Note how much time each activity requires (in minutes) in the *right* column.

Here's an example routine designed to support the intention of feeling more relaxed:

- Shower (10 minutes)
- Blow dry hair (15 minutes)
- Apply makeup (5 minutes)
- Eat a healthy breakfast (20 minutes)
- Perform breathing exercises (5 minutes)
- Practice mindful meditation (5 minutes)
- Write in a personal journal (15 minutes)
- Write a gratitude list (5 minutes)
- Listen to an uplifting podcast (15 minutes)

Note the allotted time for each activity. This list, written on paper, keeps you on track and ensures you get through your entire routine without having to rush.

If you're like me, you'll be tempted to skip this step. Don't. Resist the temptation. You'll find that writing down your morning routine will focus your attention. Once written, it'll serve as a daily reminder of your intentions.

[1] http://journals.sagepub.com/doi/abs/10.1177/0956797614524581

STEP 10: ADJUST YOUR ROUTINE TO ACCOMMODATE NEW CHALLENGES, GOALS, AND SCHEDULE CHANGES

 ~

Nothing stays the same forever. Schedules change. Goals change. New responsibilities surface, requiring more of your time and attention.

As your life changes, so too should your morning routine. Your routine will need an occasional tune-up to accommodate these changes.

For example, let's suppose your current morning ritual requires two hours to complete. You wake up at 5:45 a.m. to ensure you're able to get through your entire routine and leave your home by 8:00 a.m. (The extra 15 minutes provides a cushion.) This gives you plenty of time to deal with the morning commute to your office, at which you're expect to arrive at 8:30 a.m.

Now, let's say your boss asks you to arrive at 8:00 a.m. for the foreseeable future. You're left with two options:

1. Shorten your morning routine to 90 minutes. This

might entail shortening the duration of certain activities or eliminating some altogether (or both).

2. Wake up 30 minutes earlier.

The point is that you must adjust your routine to accommodate the change in your morning schedule.

Here's another example: let's say you designed your current routine to help you to lose weight. It's filled with various types of cardiovascular exercise to effect that outcome.

Suppose that after three months of performing this routine, you've successfully reached your target weight. *Losing* weight is no longer your goal, or intention. *Maintaining* your weight is. You need to adjust your morning routine to accommodate your new intention. To that end, you might replace the cardiovascular exercise with doing yoga, taking a walk, and eating a low-carb breakfast.

The point is to update your morning ritual as your circumstances and goals change. That way, you're able to leverage your mornings to their full advantage.

Here's What To Do Right Now

In Step 1, we identified your purpose for having a morning ritual. In subsequent steps, we created a routine designed to match that intention.

Review your purpose. Think about it carefully. Note whether it's still important to you. Is it still a daily priority? If it is, then stick to your current routine. If your intention has changed, go through Steps 2 through 9 again to create a new routine that's better suited to it.

Next, review your morning responsibilities, particularly those that require you to be somewhere at a certain time. Have they changed recently? Have new obligations been imposed on you? Have new circumstances arisen, leaving you with less time in the morning? If so, be proactive in making adjustments to your routine.

I recommend doing this once a week. Pick a day - I like Sundays for this task - and schedule it on your calendar. Treat it like a high-priority to-do list item. That way, you can regularly monitor your morning routine, and note whether it's still a workable solution that's consistent with your intentions.

THE KEY TO SUCCESS: INCREMENTAL PROGRESS

~

I mentioned this in *Step 6: Start With A Simple Plan*. But it's important enough to repeat.

The most effective way to adopt any new habit or routine is to do so gradually, in small steps. As Shakespeare wrote in *Romeo and Juliet*, "Wisely, and slow. They stumble that run fast."

That's been the story of my life when I've adopted new habits, including my morning rituals. If I try to change too many things at once, I'm almost guaranteed to fail. On the other hand, if I change one thing at a time, the changes tend to stick.

I'll bet you can relate. Think back to the last time you tried to make radical changes in your lifestyle. Were you able to make them all at once? Or did you end up abandoning most of them in the weeks that followed?

If the latter is true, you're not alone. That's the experience most of us have.

Introducing change always produces resistance. The bigger the change, the more resistance you'll confront. That's the reason

I advocate starting with a simple morning routine and adding to it incrementally. Allow your mind and body to acclimate to each new activity.

It's fine to have big plans for changing the manner in which you spend your mornings. But don't feel you have to enact all of your plans in one fell swoop. Go slowly. Implement one change at a time. I guarantee you'll experience more *lasting* success.

Coming Up Next...

In *Part III*, we'll explore common obstacles people face when they implement new, purposeful morning routines. There's a good chance you'll confront at least a few of them. I'm going to show you how to address them productively.

PART III

HOW TO DEAL WITH CHALLENGES AND MISSTEPS

~

You're going to make mistakes. You're also going to confront challenges. You're going to face stumbling blocks that can, in the moment, be profoundly discouraging and frustrating.

It's important to proceed with these expectations. When obstacles threaten to derail your new morning routine, you won't instantly feel defeated. Instead, having expected to face them, you'll be able to address them with reason and practicality.

Part III is short. But don't be fooled by its brevity. As you confront challenges when implementing your morning routines, you may find it to be one of the most important sections of this action guide.

WHAT IF YOU MISS A DAY?

~

No one's perfect. Even the most committed dieters occasionally eat junk food. Even the most devoted fitness enthusiasts skip the gym once in a while. Even the staunchest productivity experts waste time on Facebook every now and then.

From time to time, there will be mornings that slip past you. You might inadvertently sleep through your alarm, leaving you with insufficient time to perform your morning routine. Or an emergency might arise that requires your time and attention, forcing you to abandon your routine.

Missing a day, while not ideal, shouldn't cause you concern. If you're responsible for causing circumstances that force you to skip your morning routine - for example, you slept through your alarm - forgive yourself. Again, no one's perfect. We're human and make mistakes.

The important thing is that we learn from our mistakes, and make changes to enjoy greater success down the road. For example, if you slept through your alarm, try to identify the reason.

Have you accumulated a massive sleep debt as a result of going to bed too late each night? Or are you overly stressed, and thus mentally exhausted?

Once you identify the root cause that explains why you missed your morning routine, you can make changes to resolve it. For example, you can plan to go to sleep earlier or practice mindful meditation to destress.

What About Life's Inevitable Curve Balls?

Sometimes, of course, life gets in the way, erecting unanticipated obstacles. To that end, you may be forced to abandon your morning routine for the day through no fault of your own.

For example, suppose your child becomes seriously ill and needs to be taken to the hospital. Missing your morning routine is the least of your concerns. The wellbeing of your child naturally takes precedence.

Having said that, some folks are so inflexible with themselves that such circumstances are small consolation, even though they have no control over them. Missing their morning routine nags at their consciences.

When life throws a curve ball, the healthiest, most practical response is to adapt to it. Accept the interruption to your morning, knowing you have little control over it. Let it go and move on.

In fact, it's helpful to recognize the inherent silver lining. While an unanticipated disruption can negatively impact your entire day, it also demonstrates why your morning ritual is important to you. It allows you to exert control over most of your mornings in pursuit of a purposeful intention.

WHAT IF YOU HATE MORNINGS?

~

I f you're not a morning person, waking up early is bad enough. Once you've dragged yourself from the comfort of your bed, the thought of practicing yoga, going for a jog, or writing in a personal journal fills you with dread. It hangs over you like a dark cloud.

Given this mindset, how can you possibly get up early and perform a morning routine, day after day?

Here's what I found to be true in my life: success in becoming a morning person is 90% attitude and 10% showing up. Our attitudes define who we are and what we're able to accomplish. They also determine our limitations.

This is great news because *you* control your outlook. *You're* the hero or heroine of your life, and responsible for how you see yourself. This means you can adjust your perspective to overcome bad habits and adopt new ones that help you to accomplish your goals.

For example, suppose you've repeatedly claimed over the years that you're "not a morning person." This is how you see yourself. You've written an invisible script that defines this trait as part of your character.

In this case, becoming a morning person starts with changing this script. Once you begin to see yourself as a morning person, you'll find it easier to wake up early. You'll be more excited to get the day started, especially after you've identified your intentions.

This script change isn't an overnight process. Nor will it be easy. You'll almost certainly face internal resistance as you retrain your mind to accept this new identity.

But once you change your outlook about mornings, you'll find that transforming yourself into a morning person isn't nearly as difficult as you had imagined. You may even discover that you *thrive* during the morning hours.

Remember, you're the director of your life story. You can rewrite the script in any way you choose. If you currently hate mornings, ask yourself the reason. Then, challenge the claim to see if it's valid. It's possible that you're "not a morning person" simply because you've repeatedly told yourself as much, conditioning your brain in the process.

WHAT IF YOU WAKE UP EXHAUSTED?

∼

I f you feel exhausted when you wake up in the morning, you're in good company. Research shows that 40% of U.S. adults wake up at least once, and often as many as three times, a week feeling tired. Thirty-eight percent experience feelings of fatigue upon waking four times a week.[1]

The problem is, if you're chronically tired, you're going to find it difficult to get out of bed when your alarm goes off. And if you're unable to get up at the time you planned to do so, you won't have enough time to perform your morning routine. So it's worth investigating the root cause of your exhaustion.

Many folks who regularly feel tired upon waking simply don't get enough sleep. If you're facing this problem, the solution may be as simple as going to bed earlier. I also recommend you reread the section *10 Quick Tips To Ensure You Get A Good Night's Sleep (Every Night!)*.

Having said that, there are other reasons you may be feeling exhausted in the morning, and they have nothing to do with the number of hours you sleep each night. Many people sleep eight hours and *still* feel tired when they wake up. The aforementioned research found that 27% of U.S. adults report as much.

What's causing this problem? What factors are contributing to this feeling of exhaustion, even after folks get the recommended amount of sleep?

Here are a few possibilities:

- **Poor sleep quality.** It doesn't matter if you're in bed for eight hours if your brain isn't experiencing full sleep cycles.
- **Bedroom devoid of natural light.** Waking up in the dark confuses the brain, making it think it should still be sleeping. (Light and darkness are cues for our circadian rhythms, which dictate our sleep patterns.)
- **Use of gadgets right before bedtime.** Phones and tablets emit blue light, which smothers the release of the hormone melatonin.[2] Melatonin promotes sleep.
- **Alcohol consumption before bedtime.** A bottle of merlot might make you feel drowsy. But it also limits the amount of REM (rapid eye movement) sleep you get while sleeping.[3]
- **Stress.** Did you have an argument with your spouse before going to bed? Is your job in jeopardy? Did a loved one pass away recently? These circumstances increase your stress levels, which can play havoc with your ability to sleep soundly.[4]

If you regularly feel exhausted when you wake up, try to identify the reason. Don't assume things are fine just because you're in bed for eight hours a night. There may be other issues preventing you from enjoying the *restful* slumber you need to feel energized upon waking.

If you're unable to pinpoint the reason (or reasons) on your own, seek the help of a sleep expert. It's that important.

[1] https://today.yougov.com/news/2015/06/02/sleep-and-dreams/

[2]   http://www.health.harvard.edu/staying-healthy/blue-light-has-a-dark-side

[3]   http://www.health.harvard.edu/staying-healthy/blue-light-has-a-dark-side

[4] https://www.ncbi.nlm.nih.gov/pmc/articles/PMC3538178/

WHAT IF YOU'RE A HABITUAL SNOOZER?

~

Many people treat the snooze button on their alarm clocks and phones as if it were a trusted friend. In a way, it's the first "friend" they greet in the morning as they reach over groggily and hit the button.

But the snooze feature is most certainly *not* your friend. In fact, it can wreck your morning and negatively impact your entire day.

Most folks hit snooze because they want to get a few more minutes of sleep. But it's important to realize these extra minutes are unhelpful. You won't feel more rested when the alarm goes off again in seven or eight minutes. Why? Because waking up interrupts your sleep cycle.

When you "hit snooze" to enjoy a few more minutes of sleep, your brain doesn't simply resume its progress through the interrupted cycle. It must start a *new* cycle. Given that your snooze alarm will go off in less than 10 minutes, there isn't enough time to complete the deep-sleep stages of the new cycle.

That's the reason you feel just as groggy when the snooze alarm goes off as you felt when the initial alarm woke you up.

In short, hitting the snooze button, whether once or repeatedly, isn't doing you any favors. On the contrary, it eats into time you can otherwise spend doing your morning routine. That, of course, will negatively affect the rest of your day.

If you're a habitual snoozer, how can you break the habit? How can you train yourself to ignore the snooze button and get out of bed when your alarm goes off the first time? Try the following:

- **Set your alarm clock or phone out of reach.** If your clock or phone is positioned next to you - for example, on a nightstand near your bed - it'll be tempting to hit the snooze button when the alarm goes off. Position it on the other side of your bedroom. If you're forced to get out of bed to turn the alarm off, you'll be more inclined to start your morning.

- **Review your "why" the night before.** In *Part II: 10 Steps To Creating A Perfect Morning Routine*, we identified your reason (or reasons) for developing and performing a morning ritual. Mull this reason, or intention, over before going to bed. What do you want to achieve and why do you want to achieve it? If you're focused on your goal, you'll be more excited to get up in the morning to pursue it.

- **Wake up at the same time each morning.** We covered this in the section *10 Quick Tips To Ensure You Get A Good Night's Sleep (Every Night!)*. But it's worth repeating in the context of training yourself to avoid hitting the snooze button. Getting up at the same time each morning anchors that time in your brain. It sets your internal clock. After awhile, you may find that

you no longer even need your alarm to wake you up;
you'll wake up naturally at your desired time.

- **Train yourself to spring out of bed.** This practice may
sound strange, but I urge you to give it a try. Jump out
of bed the moment your alarm goes off. Open your
eyes and take a few deep breaths. Recall your "why"
and be enthusiastic about pursuing it. This simple
tactic can change your entire mindset to the point that
you no longer even consider hitting the snooze button.

If you dread getting out of bed in the morning, try the four
tips I've outlined above. You might find that you're not only less
inclined to hit snooze, but actually excited to get your day started.

WHAT IF YOU HAVE YOUNG CHILDREN?

～

I f you have kids, you know firsthand the challenges of getting them ready in the morning. You need to wake them up, and get them dressed, fed, and out the door in time to catch the bus to school. If you drop them off at school yourself, or take them to daycare, you'll need to take into account the associated commute time when planning your morning.

There's reason to celebrate when everything goes according to plan. In most households with young children, small delays are to be expected. They're part of the territory. Kids dawdle and lose focus. Unfortunately, small delays can quickly accumulate and force you to scramble to meet inflexible time constraints.

For example, your kids might need to arrive at school by 8:20 a.m. That time isn't negotiable. The problem is, everything leading up to it, from getting your kids out of bed to getting them dressed and fed, is variable in terms of how much time is needed. If your kids dally while getting dressed, that leaves them less time to eat breakfast. If they goof off while brushing their teeth, that leaves them less time to put their pajamas away.

It's no wonder parents feel so harried in the morning!

If you face these circumstances, how can you make time for your *own* morning routine? What can you do to ensure you're getting the time *you* need to prepare for a successful day?

The simplest way to carve out time for yourself in the morning is to wake up earlier. If you wake up before everyone else in your household, you'll enjoy quiet time that won't be interrupted.

Getting up earlier isn't something you should attempt without a plan. The last thing you want to do is rob yourself of quality sleep just to perform your personal morning ritual. Doing so will only result in a sleep debt that you'll eventually have to repay. If you want to wake up earlier, go to sleep earlier and take steps to make sure you enjoy *quality* sleep.

The bigger challenge is streamlining your kids' morning routine to minimize avoidable delays. I recommend doing the following the night before:

- Lay out your kids' clothes.
- Prepare your kids' lunches.
- Make sure your kids' backpacks contain the proper books, papers, and materials.
- Set out plates, dishes, and glasses for the following morning's breakfast.
- Write down your kids' morning routine so they'll know what to do and in what order to do it (e.g. make the bed, get dressed, put their pajamas away, eat breakfast, brush their teeth, put their shoes on, etc., in that order).
- Forbid nonessential activities. Don't allow your children to play video games, text friends, or watch cartoons in the morning.

The fact that you have young children shouldn't stop you from maintaining your *own* morning routine. By planning carefully the night before and keeping your kids on task after they wake up, you can get them ready and still have plenty of time for yourself.

WHAT IF YOU LACK WILLPOWER?

∾

S uppose you've tried to incorporate a morning routine and repeatedly failed to follow through on it. You stay in bed and hit the snooze button. By the time you finally get up, there's no time to run through your planned ritual. You have to scramble just to leave the house on time.

You might tell yourself, "*I need to have more willpower in the morning.*" But that's untrue. Willpower isn't the solution.

Willpower is one of the most misunderstood aspects of our lives. And because we misunderstand how it works, we tend to needlessly punish ourselves when we fail.

If we're dieting and give in to the temptation to eat a donut, we berate ourselves. If we're trying to stick to a daily exercise regimen and decide to watch TV instead of going to the gym, we reprimand ourselves. If we're trying to adopt a new morning routine and decide to stay in bed rather than perform it, we feel like abject failures.

And the personal rebuke is always the same: "*I need to have more willpower.*"

The problem is, willpower is like a tank of gas. You use a little each time you make a decision to forgo one option for another. This depletion occurs throughout the day until the tank is empty.

Willpower is also unreliable. While we have more of it in the morning than we do in the evening, we may not have enough to overcome resistance and take purposeful action. It's unwise to depend on it.

So if more willpower isn't the solution, what *is*?

Simple: creating a habit. When you do something over and over with consistency, the behavior becomes ingrained. At that point, you don't need willpower.

For example, you brush your teeth every morning. Because you've been doing so for years, it's a deeply-rooted habit. You don't have to consider the benefits of doing it. You just do it. You don't need willpower to make it happen.

This is the reason it's important to make your morning ritual a *habit*. Doing so completely eliminates the need to depend on willpower, a finite and unreliable resource.

How long will it take you to adopt a habit to the point that it becomes ingrained? That's difficult to say with certainty. It varies from person to person. Research shows it can take anywhere between 18 to 254 days, depending on the individual.[1]

Research also shows that *environment* plays a major role in how we make choices between competing options.[2] In short, we can design an environment that supports our efforts to develop the morning-routine habit.

We touched on this idea in the section *Step 7: Streamline Your Morning Routine*. There, I gave the example of placing your running shoes at the side of your bed. Doing so reduces resistance to going jogging (if that's part of your routine). I also advised putting a glass of water on your nightstand. Doing so make it easy to hydrate immediately upon waking.

Here's the takeaway: you don't need willpower to maintain your morning routine. You just need to make your routine a habit. With time and consistent execution, the behavior will become so deeply rooted that your mind will want to take action naturally upon waking.

Let's close this section with a relevant quote from Aristotle:

 "We are what we repeatedly do. Excellence then, is not an act, but a habit."

[1] http://onlinelibrary.wiley.com/doi/10.1002/ejsp.674/abstract

[2] https://www.ncbi.nlm.nih.gov/pubmed/22390518

WHAT IF YOU WORK DURING
ODD HOURS?

~

Not everyone has a normal work schedule. Some people work odd or irregular hours. Others have responsibilities that prevent them from going to bed and waking up at the same time each day.

If that describes your circumstances, is it still possible for you to incorporate a morning routine? The answer, of course, is yes.

Even if you work nontraditional hours - for example, the graveyard shift - you're still maintaining *some* type of schedule. You go to sleep at a certain time and you wake up at a certain time. Incorporating a morning routine is just a matter of accommodating your schedule.

For example, suppose you work the night shift. Your shift begins at 11:00 p.m. and ends at 8:00 a.m. If you go to bed shortly after returning home (e.g. 9:00 a.m.), your "mornings" start around 5:00 p.m. (assuming you sleep for eight hours). If you prefer to eat a meal and do errands after your shift, and go to sleep at noon, your "mornings" start around 8:00 p.m.

In both circumstances, you're still keeping a schedule. It's just a non-traditional one. As such, you would perform your morning routine according to that schedule. It's a simple matter of shifting the time frame. Instead of doing it at 5:00 *a.m.*, you'd do it at 5:00 *p.m.* (as an example).

Maintaining a morning routine with an *irregular* schedule is a bit more complicated. Having to report to work at different times each day of the week can wreak havoc on any sense of order you enjoy in your life.

Here, routines are more important than ever. It's just a matter of carefully planning them.

Even if your schedule is irregular, you probably know when you need to report throughout the week. Moreover, your schedule is unlikely to vary wildly from day to day (e.g. starting your shift at 8:00 a.m. on Monday and 8:00 p.m. on Tuesday). If it did, mental and physical exhaustion would make it impossible to sustain over the long run.[I] Given this, you can still maintain a consistent morning routine.

For example, take a look at the following irregular work schedule.

- Monday: 8:00 a.m. - 5:00 p.m.
- Tuesday: 10:00 a.m. - 7:00 p.m.
- Wednesday: 12:00 p.m. - 8:00 p.m.
- Thursday: 7:00 a.m. - 4:00 p.m.
- Friday: 9:00 a.m. - 6:00 p.m.

Let's say you've created the following morning routine, which requires 120 minutes (two hours):

- Brush teeth and use the restroom (5 minutes)
- Shower (10 minutes)
- Blow dry hair (15 minutes)
- Perform stretching exercises (5 minutes)
- Go for a jog (15 minutes)

- Write in a personal journal (20 minutes)
- Get dressed (5 minutes)
- Eat breakfast (15 minutes)
- Meditate (5 minutes)
- Morning commute (25 minutes)

Take another look at the irregular work schedule above. The earliest you have to report to work is 7:00 a.m. (Thursday). In order to complete your morning routine, you'd need to get out of bed at 5:00 a.m.

Make 5:00 a.m. your normal wakeup time. Be consistent throughout the week. Even though you don't need to report to work until noon on Wednesday, you should still get up at 5:00 a.m. on that day, too. Doing so trains your brain to adhere to a consistent sleep pattern. This, in turn, will keep your internal clock on track.

If you get up at 5:00 a.m., you'll have plenty of time to perform your morning routine regardless of the day. Your irregular schedule won't be an obstacle.

To be sure, working odd hours can be a challenge when adopting a morning routine. But it's a challenge that can be easily addressed. All it takes is a bit of planning and flexibility.

Coming Up Next...

Part IV will explore the morning routines of 10 incredibly successful people. You'll no doubt be familiar with many of their names. By examining how these folks spend their mornings, we'll gain better insight into how a *purposeful* morning routine can set the stage for a truly victorious day.

[1] http://oem.bmj.com/content/60/suppl_1/i47.full

10 MORNING ROUTINES OF HIGHLY-SUCCESSFUL PEOPLE

∾

If you talk to successful entrepreneurs, ambitious athletes, high-level executives, and business owners about how they spend their mornings, you'll notice a common theme. They spend their time with purpose. They know what they want to accomplish during the day and stick to morning routines that help them do so.

Some of these go-getters start their days much earlier than others. Some engage in activities that would surely cause their peers to cringe. The point is that each of them has a carefully-planned morning ritual that works for him or her.

It's worth studying how these ultra-productive high performers spend their mornings, if only to see how their routines vary. As we review their routines, we'll uncover ideas you may want to incorporate into your own morning ritual.

Don't be afraid to experiment. That's the most efficient way to identify what works best for *you*.

First up: author and motivational speaker Tony Robbins.

#1: TONY ROBBINS'S PRIMING TECHNIQUE

Tony Robbins is known for his high-intensity stage manner. People who have attended his seminars claim his energy is contagious.

But Robbins does more than merely conduct seminars. He coaches high-performance athletes, top executives, and even high-profile investment advisors. And along the way, he's managed to write and sell millions of books.

To say Robbins is an overachiever would be an understatement.

He calls his morning routine "priming." He goes through it regardless of whether he has an hour available to him or 10 minutes. In fact, he says,

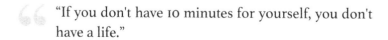 "If you don't have 10 minutes for yourself, you don't have a life."

There are three components to his ritual:

1. Breathing
2. Conveying gratitude
3. Praying / Meditating

Robbins practices a yoga exercise called Kapalabhati Pranayama. It hones breath control. Sitting upright, he breathes in deeply through his nostrils, and then exhales through his mouth in a short burst. Robbins performs three sets of 30 breaths each morning.

Following his breathing exercises, Robbins takes a few moments to express his gratitude about three specific things in his life. It sets his outlook for the day. He notes that it's difficult to be anxious, angry, or resentful when you feel grateful for something.

After expressing his gratitude, Robbins prays. He asks God for strength to get through the day and fulfill his responsibilities. He also prays for everyone he knows, from his family to his clients. Robbins points out that this part of his priming ritual doesn't necessarily have to be attached to religion. It's more of a spiritual pursuit, which is likely to be experienced differently by each person.

In addition to his priming ritual, Robbins favors cryotherapy. It's the practice of lowering the body's temperature via exposure to liquid nitrogen. Research indicates it can reduce inflammation and pain while improving physical performance.[1]

Thoughts On Tony Robbins's Morning Routine

Robbins's priming ritual is great for two reasons. First, anyone can do it. Second, it can be done quickly. If you have 10 minutes, you can get through the entire routine.

Personally, I've found all three segments useful. I perform breathing exercises to hone my focus and lower my stress levels.

I've also found that expressing gratitude and praying put me in a positive state of mind.

I encourage you to try these three activities for yourself. Adjust to suit your preferences. For example, you don't have to perform Kapalabhati Pranayama breathing. Simply close your eyes, and inhale and exhale with purpose. Do so for three minutes and note how it makes you feel.

Do likewise with expressing gratitude and praying (or meditating). If they suit you, make them a part of your morning routine. If not, don't. Remember, the key is to design a routine that works for *you*.

What about cryotherapy? Unfortunately, it isn't an option for most of us, and certainly not on a daily basis. Few of us have access to the technology. But there *are* things you can do to simulate the experience. For example, you can take a cold shower or ice bath in the morning.

Note that neither practice is for the fainthearted. It can be a shock to your system. Personally, I'm content to drink cold water.

[1] https://www.ncbi.nlm.nih.gov/pmc/articles/PMC3956737/

#2: GARY VAYNERCHUK'S 3-HOUR DAILY PREP

~

There are a lot of ways to describe Gary Vaynerchuk. He's an entrepreneur, but that label doesn't do him justice. In truth, he's a *serial* entrepreneur. He's launched a wine business, growing it into a $60 million venture within five years. He launched Wine Library TV, and went on to record 1,000 episodes before closing it down. He went on to launch VayerMedia, a digital marketing agency that has become one of the most sought-after firms among the Fortune 500.

But Vaynerchuck isn't just an entrepreneur. He's also a New York Times bestselling author, professional investor (through his firm RSE Ventures), and public speaker.[1]

And he has two young children.

Vaynerchuck regularly works 18-hour days to keep up with his family, multiple businesses, and other interests. He's noted in the past that "every minute counts, so my schedule is planned down *to the second*." That means he needs to make the most of his mornings.

He follows the same ritual, which takes nearly three hours to complete.

First, he wakes up at 6:00 a.m. regardless of whether it's a weekday, weekend, or national holiday. He immediately grabs his phone and heads to the bathroom for his morning constitutional. There, he looks through news headlines, email, his Twitter feed, sports articles, and material relevant to his digital agency. Then, he hops over to Instagram to look at new pictures uploaded by his friends.

Next, he works out. He spends between 45 minutes and an hour with a personal trainer. His goal is twofold: minimize body fat and maximize muscle gain. He prefers to keep a lean physique, believing it helps him to get through his 18-hour days.

Finally, he spends time with his family. Vaynerchuk openly admits that he only spends five to 10 minutes with his kids in the morning during the week. But he spends hours with them during the weekends and vacations.

By the time he kisses his children goodbye, it's nearly 9:00 a.m., and he's off to the first meeting of his busy day.

Thoughts On Gary Vaynerchuk's Morning Routine

The first part of Vaynerchuk's morning ritual is devoted to information consumption. He consumes a massive amount of reading material while he's in the bathroom.

Personally, I've found that reading news stories and articles related to my businesses in the morning to be distracting. It erodes my focus. Having said that, if I were juggling as many projects as Vaynerchuk and those projects required constant attention, I might follow the same ritual. I'd try to overcome my inclination toward distraction.

This practice might resonate with you. If so, I encourage you to "test drive" it as part of your own morning routine. It if helps you, keep it. If not, get rid of it.

Physical exercise, the second part of Vaynerchuk's ritual, doesn't have to be about minimizing fat and maximizing muscle. It could be a simple cardio routine that raises your heart rate and increases your alertness. Any form of body movement counts. Moreover, don't feel as if you need to spend an hour doing it.

My morning routine includes five minutes of stretching. That works for me. Experiment to find what works for you.

If you have children, the third part of Vaynerchuk's ritual may strike a chord. Spending quality time with your kids in the morning, even if only for a few minutes, does more than just strengthen the connection you share with them. It can improve your mood and disposition. That, in turn, can make the entire day more rewarding.

[1]   https://www.ted.com/talks/gary_vaynerchuk_do_what_you_love_no_excuses

#3: TIM FERRISS'S 5-PART REGIMEN

~

Tim Ferriss is the author of the acclaimed #1 New York Times bestseller *The 4-Hour Workweek*. Since writing the book, he's built an empire around the *4-Hour* brand, authoring several other books, giving public talks,[1] and maintaining a popular blog and podcast. Ferris is also an angel investor and consultant for some of today's largest brands, including Uber, Facebook, and Twitter. He's also an entrepreneur, journalist, and an accomplished kickboxer.

Simply put, Ferriss has a lot on his plate.

In 2016, he released *Tools of Titans*, a book that details the morning routines of the world's most successful people. Ferriss experimented with these routines and evaluated how the activities they contained affected his day. He eventually settled on five:

1. Making his bed
2. Meditation
3. Exercise
4. Hydration

5. Journaling

Ferriss starts off each morning by making his bed. He doesn't do it to keep his bedroom tidy. Rather, he does it because it gives him a sense of control. Ferriss points out that each day presents circumstances he's unable to influence. These circumstances sometimes make him feel as if he has little control over his day. But he notes about making his bed:

 "In a world full of unpredictable and uncontrolled variables, you can start your day with a tiny win. And you can also come back to something you've accomplished at the tail end of the day."

After making his bed, he practices transcendental meditation for 21 minutes. He spends the first 60 seconds fidgeting and getting into the right frame of mind. The next 20 minutes are spent reciting a mantra that helps him to block out distracting thoughts and clear his head.

Following his meditation, Ferriss exercises. He doesn't spend an hour doing so like Gary Vaynerchuk. Instead, he simply moves his body for 30 seconds. He usually does so in the form of pushups and dips.

Next, Ferriss hydrates with a pot of pu-ehr tea (a fermented black tea). He adds coconut oil or caprylic acid, claiming the brain craves the type of fat found in both.

Lastly, he writes in a journal. He spends five to 10 minutes reviewing his accomplishments and expressing gratitude for the blessings in his life. He calls this activity "therapeutic intervention."

Ferriss isn't a perfectionist. He also realizes that life can sometimes thwart his intentions. While his goal is to perform all five activities each morning, he considers the morning a success if he manages to perform three of them.

Thoughts On Tim Ferriss's Morning Routine

I love Ferriss's routine for two reasons. First, it's simple. Anyone can do it.

Second, it's flexible. You can meditate for three minutes or 20 minutes. You can exercise for 30 seconds or half an hour. If you don't enjoy tea, hydrate with water. His routine is completely adaptable, putting you in control.

Much of Ferriss's routine is similar to the one I use to prepare for a day of writing. For example, I make the bed in the morning, and do so for the same reason he does: it's a small win that I control. It gives me the sense that I have influence over something. It's a small thing, but for me, it has a large effect on my attitude.

Ferriss claims that 80% of the people he's interviewed regarding their morning routines meditate. He's found the practice valuable in helping him to control his emotions. I've experienced the same thing. Although I prefer mindful meditation to transcendental meditation, I've found it's effective for releasing tension and managing the way I respond to adverse circumstances.

Again, I recommend you experiment with it. The practice may seem strange at first if you're unaccustomed to it, but you might find that it's a great addition to your morning routine.

I love Ferriss's approach to early-morning exercise. He doesn't do it get into shape. Nor does he spend a lot of time on it. Instead, he uses it to focus his mind and get his blood pumping, and spends less than a minute doing so. His "real" workout happens in the evening.

Personally, I enjoy stretching exercises. Doing them makes me feel more limber and helps to clear my head. You might enjoy doing some other type of physical activity, such as pushups, squats, or rowing. Again, experiment to see what works for you.

Ferriss claims that drinking tea helps him to prime his mind.

He's thus better able to focus and set the day's priorities. If you don't enjoy tea, you can - and arguably should - still incorporate hydration into your morning routine. I prefer water when I wake up followed by a Caffè Americano at Starbucks. You might prefer a glass of orange juice, soy milk, or unsweetened cranberry juice. Test a few beverages and monitor their effects. Note how they make you feel.

Ferriss claims journaling makes him happier and reduces his anxiety. It gives him a chance to reflect on his life, particularly on the things for which he's grateful. He's able to set aside his Type A personality and take a few minutes to truly appreciate his circumstances.

I don't write in a personal journal these days. Most of my writing is focused on creating materials for others to read (e.g. books, blogs, emails, etc.). Having said that, I relate to the benefits of journaling that Ferriss highlights. One of my favorite things to do is to sit in my car and just think about my place in life. I think about my goals, my accomplishments, and the things I'm grateful for. This practice may sound strange, but it always refreshes my outlook.

If you've never journaled, give it a try. Write about the emotions you're experiencing; jot down ideas you'd like to pursue in the future; note things you're grateful for.

Whatever you write is for your eyes only. Don't be concerned that someone else will read it and poke fun. Give yourself the freedom to write down all of your thoughts, even if they might seem odd to others. I'm willing to bet you'll find the activity both invigorating and therapeutic.

[1]   https://www.ted.com/talks/tim_ferriss_s-mash_fear_learn_anything

#4: KEVIN O'LEARY'S THREE-PRIORITY MORNING

~

Kevin O'Leary has a busy schedule. In addition to being a major presence on the television show *Shark Tank*, he runs an investment firm (O'Leary Financial), a beverage company (O'Leary Fine Wines), and is a regular contributor to multiple radio stations. He's also written three books. And as if he's not busy enough, he recently entered politics.

How does O'Leary handle such a demanding schedule? He relies on his morning routine. He claims it boosts his productivity and gets him through the day.

He wakes up early, usually before 5:45 a.m., and starts the day on his exercise bike. While riding, he peruses reports from the Asian and European bond markets. When he finishes his cycling workout - it usually lasts an hour - he heads to the office.

Once he arrives at his office, the core of his routine begins. He focuses 100% of his attention on a 3-item to-do list. The list is prepared the night before so he doesn't have to waste precious time in the morning to create it.

O'Leary ignores *everything* until he completes the three items on his to-do list. He doesn't read or respond to emails or texts. He doesn't take calls. He doesn't watch television. And he doesn't take meetings.

According to O'Leary, this one tactic has been instrumental in catapulting his productivity. He cautions against adding more than three items to the list. He claims doing so is likely to lead to overwhelm and failure. He's found that three is the ideal number.

Only *after* he completes his 3-item to-do list does he check his email, respond to texts, return phone calls, and take meetings.

Thoughts On Kevin O'Leary's Morning Routine

The beauty of O'Leary's morning routine is its simplicity. He works out while taking the pulse of the international bond markets. Then, he works on his morning to-do list, which always contains three items.

Importantly, his morning routine at the office is hyper-focused and purposeful. Everything is placed on the back burner while he devotes himself to addressing the three priorities on his morning to-do list.

Like many people who maintain demanding schedules, O'Leary exercises in the morning. He knows he's likely to forego working out if he doesn't do it immediately after waking.

Exercise is one of the most consistent elements in the morning routines of highly-successful people. These folks claim it makes them feel more alert, more creative, and more energetic. They also note that exercising in the morning improves their self-discipline.

I recommend you try it if you haven't yet done so. Remember, you don't need to spend hours at the gym. Nor do you need to work up a sweat. Start with a few stretches. Add a few pushups. Do a few squats.

If doing these exercises makes you feel better, add them to

your normal routine. Then, gradually increase the duration or intensity until you optimize the experience for your personal circumstances.

O'Leary's 3-item to-do list is a great way to start the productive part of your morning. Three is small enough so that the list won't seem daunting. At the same time, completing three high-priority tasks before the day begins can make you feel unstoppable. Each completed item is a win, which will inspire you to attack the rest of your day.

#5: FRAN TARKENTON'S "BRAIN-FEED" DRILL

⌇

Fran Tarkenton made a name for himself as a professional football player. He appeared on the gridiron for an impressive 18 seasons, during which he broke every major record in the NFL. He finally hung up his cleats in 1978, and was inducted into the Pro Football Hall of Fame in 1986.

Football wasn't Tarkenton's only interest. In addition to becoming a popular sports commentator, he co-hosted the popular reality television show *That's Incredible*. He also founded a software company (Tarkenton Software), a consulting agency (GoSmallBiz), and a financial services firm (Tarkenton Financial). Along the way, Tarkenton has written numerous books.

Like the other high achievers profiled in this section of *Morning Makeover*, Tarkenton keeps a demanding schedule. He considers his morning routine to be vital to his success. He notes:

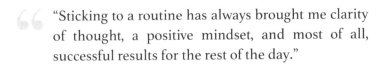
"Sticking to a routine has always brought me clarity of thought, a positive mindset, and most of all, successful results for the rest of the day."

Tarkenton's morning routine consists of three main activities:

1. Providing care to others
2. Fueling his mind
3. Tending to his body

For Tarkenton, providing care comes in the form of feeding his dogs and taking them for a run. He attends to their needs before attending to his own. Doing so is important to him as it puts him in a giving frame of mind.

After returning home, he sits down and enjoys a massive infusion of information. He reads multiple newspapers, perusing stories both domestic and foreign, liberal and conservative. He devours business articles and reads the sports sections. He even studies material that he finds boring.

His purpose is to feed his brain with a diverse set of outlooks. He claims doing so gives him a broader perspective and helps him to think better.

Following his "brain feed," Tarkenton attends to his body. He puts on his Fitbit, and does a light workout while watching the latest business news. After his workout, he hydrates and eats a nutritious breakfast composed of an assortment of berries.

Tarkenton considers nutrition and exercise to be paramount to his longevity and quality of life as he enters his senior years. He also credits both for his ability to think clearly, which he considers essential for managing his business interests and maintaining his demanding schedule.

Thoughts On Fran Tarkenton's Morning Routine

Tarkenton's stance on caring for others before attending to his own needs is intriguing. Studies show that providing care to others offers psychological benefits for the caregiver, such as a greater sense of well-being.[1] Whether you're taking care of an elderly parent, making sure your kids are properly fed before they leave for school, or taking your dog outside for a quick walk, providing care can be a fantastic way to start the day!

Unlike Tarkenton, I avoid the news during my morning routine. In fact, I purposely avoid the news throughout the day as I've learned it does little to improve my focus or outlook.

Having said that, I understand Tarkenton's point of view. He reads multiple newspapers to broaden his perspective. That can be a valuable exercise for some people, particularly those inclined to hold personal biases. For example, Tarkenton purposely reads articles written by liberal journalists despite his conservative leanings.

In my opinion, everyone can benefit from the third part of Tarkenton's morning routine: taking care of his body. Exercise not only raises your metabolism, reduces your stress, and gives you energy, but it also increases your alertness and improves your self-discipline. Additionally, it gives you a greater sense of control over your day since *you* dictate the format and duration of your workout.

Eating a nutritious breakfast is also recommended. Protein-rich foods will help regulate your blood sugar levels and keep your energy up. That, in turn, will help you to maintain focus later in the day.

[1]   http://bmcpublichealth.biomedcentral.com/articles/10.1186/1471-2458-13-773

6: SCOTT ADAMS'S 20-MINUTE AUTOPILOT SYSTEM

~

S cott Adams is the brain behind *Dilbert*, one of the most successful comic strips in the U.S. But the daily comic isn't the only thing on Adams's plate. He's authored several books, a few of which have appeared on the New York Times bestseller list. And he recently launched a new startup company (CalendarTree.com).

In order for Adams to work effectively each day, whether that means writing and drawing a new *Dilbert* comic, penning a new book, or managing his startup, he must be able to think creatively. That's a tall order for someone who has produced more than 10,000 comics since 1989, the year *Dilbert* debuted.

Adams relies heavily on his morning routine. It's surprisingly simple. He wakes up at 5:00 a.m. By 5:10 a.m., he's at his desk, drinking a cup of coffee while enjoying a protein bar (he says the two tastes are amazing together). There, he waits for inspiration to strike. This routine takes 20 minutes.

While he waits, he reads the news. He prefers to read upbeat stories about business and technology, and avoids the drudgery of political news.

According to Adams, his morning ritual has a single purpose: to put himself on autopilot so his mind will be free to fully leverage creativity when it arrives.

He notes that he's unable to *summon* creativity. All he can do is "set an attractive trap and wait." Setting that trap entails sitting patiently at his desk with his cup of joe and protein snack, like a hunter.

Adams is meticulous about following the same steps, in the same order, each morning. He's been doing it for years. He claims his routine has not only improved his creativity, but has also boosted his productivity.

That's important to Adams because his creative juices usually stop flowing by late morning. For this reason, he tries to squeeze as much mileage as possible from his early-morning hours.

Thoughts On Scott Adams's Morning Routine

Although Adams sets his alarm for 5:00 a.m., he sometimes wakes up as early as 3:30 a.m. He considers that "close enough." Rather than going back to sleep, he gets out of bed and starts his day.

I advise against doing this. If you regularly wake up before your alarm goes off, it's worth investigating the reason. For example, are you anxious or stressed about something? Or did you consume caffeine before bedtime, making it difficult to sleep peacefully?

You've presumably set your alarm to go off at a time that allows you to enjoy a full night's rest (seven or eight hours). Getting up 90 minutes earlier would infringe upon that rest. Over time, that will produce a sleep debt that affects your cognitive performance.

To his credit, Adams admits his approach may be less than ideal. He told BusinessInsider.com:

 "I'll sleep when I'm dead, which might be soon; science tells us that averaging four hours of sleep per night is unhealthy."

Adams postpones exercise until after lunchtime. He's found that working out in the morning does little to stimulate his creativity, which is his top priority.

This is a good example of how one person's routine may be a poor fit for another person. For example, I've found that doing stretching exercises boosts my creativity. Different strokes for different folks. Given the volume of work Adams has produced, as well as its success, there's no arguing that his approach works for *him*.

As noted, Adams starts each day with a cup of coffee. Most of us can relate to this. We've experienced the positive effects of consuming caffeine in the morning firsthand. In fact, some of us can't live without it (or are afraid to try). Science seems to support its use. Research shows it can improve mood, increase mental performance, and boost alertness.[1] [2] [3]

A Quick Note About Coffee

If you're like millions of other people (including Adams), you drink coffee as part of your morning routine. Perhaps you've been doing so for years. If that's the case, there's a chance your caffeine consumption, based on habit, is suboptimal. Be willing to experiment.

For example, if you're currently drinking 40 ounces of coffee each morning, reduce the amount to 20 ounces. Note whether doing so has any effect on your alertness and energy. Or try taking a caffeine pill - NoDoz and Vivarin are popular brands -

with 20 ounces of water. You may find doing so makes you less jittery and better able to focus.

Many people drink coffee in the morning even though doing so causes them gastrointestinal distress. They figure the increased alertness that comes with caffeine is a good tradeoff for the physical discomfort they experience. But it's worth noting that caffeine may not be the problem; decaffeinated coffee produces similar distress in many people.

If you're in this predicament, consider replacing coffee with an energy-boosting alternative that contains caffeine. Examples include Yerba Mate Chai, espresso, and black tea. Or try non-caffeinated drinks, such as ginseng tea and pomegranate juice. Both are known to boost energy.

The idea is to be open to trying new approaches as you create a quality morning routine. That's the only way to identify which practices work best for you.

[1] https://www.ncbi.nlm.nih.gov/pubmed/22819803

[2] https://www.ncbi.nlm.nih.gov/books/NBK209050/

[3] https://www.ncbi.nlm.nih.gov/pubmed/11140366

#7: HOWARD SCHULTZ'S MOTIVATIONAL MORNING

∼

You've probably bought something from Howard Schultz even if you've never heard of him. He's the CEO of Seattle-based coffee giant Starbucks.

Starbucks is one of those rare brands that's seemingly impervious to economic trends. It continues to grow, both in size (number of stores) and revenues, year after year, regardless of whether the world is suffering an economic downturn or upswing.

It's easy to see why.

According to a 2013 survey conducted by the National Coffee Association, 83% of U.S. adults drink coffee.[1] I shudder to think how many *kids* do the same. At my local Starbucks, it's common to see teenagers buy large cups of the stuff in the morning on their way to school.

Coffee is just as popular throughout South America. In fact, it's even more popular there than it is in the U.S.[2] As you'd expect from a growth-driven CEO of a global brand, Schultz has aggressively tried to establish a foothold on that continent.

The rest of the world seems to favor tea over coffee.[2] So Schultz long ago added tea to his extensive and growing line of beverages. While he's had difficulty expanding the Starbucks brand into Europe, Africa, and the Middle East, he's enjoyed remarkable success throughout Asia. He now plans to win over the tea market in China,[3] no small feat by any measure.

All of the above is to underscore that Schultz is *busy*. Growing and managing one of the largest brands in the world is hard work.

Unsurprisingly, Schultz relies on his morning routine to prepare for the day. He claims it gives him the energy and mental fortitude to meet its inevitable challenges.

He rises at 4:30 a.m. every morning. One of the first things he often does is send motivational emails to some of his employees. Schultz considers his employees to be a core factor behind his company's success. He thus seeks to inspire them for the day.

Next, Schultz devotes an hour to exercise. He walks his three dogs and then goes for a bike ride. After returning home, he enjoys a French press coffee with his wife. Then, he heads to his office.

Schultz makes one stop along the way: Starbucks. He drops in to grab a doppio espresso macchiato (two shots of espresso with a small bit of milk). Then, with his favorite caffeinated beverage in hand, he's off to work.

Thoughts On Howard Schultz's Morning Routine

You'll no doubt notice similarities between Schultz's morning ritual and that of other successful professionals. First, he's an early riser. He takes advantage of the early hours to spend quality time alone, getting into a positive frame of mind before tackling his day.

Second, he exercises. Spending an hour riding his bike not

only keeps him fit, but also energizes him while helping to manage his stress levels.

Third, he spends time with his family. While the time is limited - he typically leaves the house by 6:00 a.m. - it's an important part of his morning. It's a period of quiet before the cacophony of his day begins.

There's a lot to love about Schultz's morning routine. For example, inspiring others can be a great opportunity to reflect on your personal values, and use them to encourage people who are important to you. Doing so can strengthen your convictions and give you the confidence to act on them.

Exercise is also an important feature from which most people can benefit. It's not necessary to spend an hour riding a bike like Schultz. Moving your body in *any* way, even for just a few minutes, can energize you and increase your alertness. As I mentioned earlier, I've found that a few minutes spent stretching is instrumental in starting my mornings on the right foot.

Spending time with your family in the morning, even if you only have a few minutes, is a good idea for numerous reasons. It strengthens the emotional bonds you share with them. It improves communication. It keeps feelings of isolation and loneliness at bay. It also has a calming effect, which can help you to manage stressful circumstances later in the day.

A Quick Reminder

None of the above is to suggest that you should adopt Schultz's morning routine as your own. As with all of the activities described in this section of *Morning Makeover*, I encourage you to examine Schultz's routine, and mine it for ideas to incorporate into your own.

If a particular practice described here resonates with you, experiment with it. Try it and monitor its effect. Keep it if it works for you and discard it if it doesn't.

Remember, the purpose of this book isn't to create a morning routine for you. It's to help *you* design a routine that perfectly complements your intentions and goals.

[1]   http://www.usatoday.com/story/money/business/2013/04/09/coffee-mania/2069335/

[2] http://www.pewresearch.org/fact-tank/2013/12/20/chart-of-the-week-coffee-and-tea-around-the-world/

[3]   https://www.bloomberg.com/news/articles/2016-09-12/starbucks-new-tea-line-chases-china-s-9-5-billion-tea-market

#8: KAT COLE'S "BODY & MIND PREP" ROUTINE

～

As president of FOCUS Brands, Kat Cole oversees a number of well-known restaurants, bakeries, and coffee shops. These include Cinnabon, Schlotzsky's, Auntie Anne's, and Seattle's Best Coffee, as well as other recognizable brands. With so many responsibilities on her plate, it's no surprise that Cole starts each day with a carefully-planned morning routine.

Cole actually has two routines. One is designed to keep her on track whenever she's on the road. It's highly systematized to help her stay disciplined. The other allows more flexibility. She performs it at home, where the freedom to modify her routine according to her daily circumstances has value.

The morning ritual Cole performs while she's traveling only requires 20 minutes. She leverages this small time frame to prepare her mind and body for the challenges she expects to face during the day.

She wakes up at 5:00 a.m. and immediately hydrates by

drinking 24 ounces of water. While she does so, she walks around her hotel room and contemplates the day.

Next, she opens her laptop and checks her calendar for scheduled meetings and events. She also reads and responds to email, and logs into Facebook and Twitter. Cole then peruses the major news websites to catch up on late-breaking stories that might affect the brands under her direction.

According to Cole, the hydration part of her routine fuels her body. Meanwhile, checking email and social media, and reading news headlines, fuels her mind.

She performs this 20-minute ritual without fail whenever she's away from home. The hour *following* this ritual, however, can progress in a variety of ways depending on the weather and her mood.

If the weather is good, Cole will often go jogging. She spends 30 minutes working up a sweat while listening to her favorite electronic dance music. Before returning to her hotel room, she stops by a café to grab a cup of coffee and enjoy the coffeehouse atmosphere.

If the weather is bad or the area near Cole's hotel is sketchy, she'll stay indoors. She exercises in her room or takes advantage of the hotel's gym (if one is available).

Cole follows a more flexible routine when she's at home. Depending on her schedule, she'll wake up anytime between 5:30 a.m. and 7:00 a.m.

She spends the first 20 minutes of her morning in the same manner as she does while traveling: hydrating, walking, and reading. She then takes shots of wheatgrass and turmeric, and follows them with a mild regimen of yoga and stretching exercises. On her way out the door, Cole grabs a high-protein snack for quick, lasting energy.

Thoughts On Kat Cole's Morning Routines

Two aspects of Cole's morning routines stand out to me. First, her initial ritual is short. It only takes 20 minutes. That's enough time for her to get into a frame of mind that prepares her to meet and overcome the challenges she'll face later in the day.

That's noteworthy. If a 20-minute routine is sufficient for Cole, who oversees several businesses, it should suffice for most of us.

This is good news if you're feeling daunted by the idea of creating a morning ritual. Start small. You may be pleasantly surprised by the extent to which a short routine can positively affect your day.

Second, Cole gives herself the freedom to modify her morning routine according to her daily circumstances. If she has a meeting at 6:30 a.m., she'll forgo jogging without regret. If her first meeting of the day is at 9:00 a.m., she might "sleep in" until 7:00 a.m. (assuming she's not on the road).

Personally, I enjoy keeping a regimented schedule. For example, like Gary Vaynerchuck, I wake up at the same time each morning, whether it's a weekday, weekend, or holiday. My routines are set in stone. That's the only way I'll stay disciplined.

But that's me. *You* might thrive with more freedom. Like Cole, you may find that adjusting your morning routine based on your daily schedule is more empowering.

As always, I encourage you to experiment and take notes. That's the only way to know for certain what works for *you*.

#9: CHERYL BACHELDER'S "PREPARE TO LEAD" RITUAL

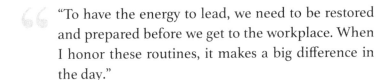

Cheryl Bachelder runs Popeyes Louisiana Kitchen, a chain comprised of over 2,500 restaurants worldwide. As its CEO, she has a lengthy list of responsibilities, including leading a large executive team.

Her schedule isn't for the fainthearted.

Bachelder admits to disliking mornings; in fact, she describes herself as a night owl. It's for this reason that she considers her morning routine especially important. It helps her to adopt a positive attitude in preparation for her day. As she recently told Inc.com:

> "To have the energy to lead, we need to be restored and prepared before we get to the workplace. When I honor these routines, it makes a big difference in the day."

One of the keys to her morning routine is music. She listens to it while performing her first activities.

She favors inspirational music, similar to the type she enjoyed listening to as a child. Her playlist includes hymns, children's songs, and other tunes that remind her of her family.

When Bachelder is on the road, she makes sure to eat a healthy breakfast of eggs, bacon, and rye toast. When she's at home, she favors steel-cut oatmeal.

Bachelder spends a significant part of her morning reading. Doing so allows her to spend quiet time reflecting on substantive issues she considers important to her role as a leader.

Once a week, she writes for her blog. She focuses on the practice of leadership in the context of serving others. Bachelder believes passionately that "servant leadership" is the most effective strategy for motivating employees to perform at their best.

Like many leaders, Bachelder considers coffee to be a crucial part of her morning. She also takes a variety of vitamins to stay healthy.

Thoughts On Cheryl Bachelder's Morning Routine

I love the fact that Bachelder uses music to get into the right frame of mind in the morning. I relate to this as I use music to the same end (albeit a different type of music for a different purpose).

Music is powerful. It can inspire us, energize us, help us to focus, and invoke emotions that might otherwise remain buried. If music isn't a part of your morning routine, I encourage you to experiment with it. Monitor its effect on you.

For example, listen to piano sonatas while reading. Does it help you to concentrate or is it a distraction? Listen to your favorite rock music while exercising. Does it make you feel more energetic? Listen to inspirational music while writing in your personal journal. Does doing so help the words flow out of you?

Years ago, I would write in silence because I assumed music would be a distraction. And for the most part, it was. I tried writing while listening to rock music, new-age instrumental music, dance music, and even country. I almost gave up. But I eventually discovered that classical music, specifically piano etudes, sharpened my focus and helped me to increase my output.

So, try it. You may stumble upon a type of music that perfectly complements certain activities you've made a part of your morning routine.

I also love that Bachelder eats breakfast each morning. It fuels her mind and body, and prepares her for the rest of her day. While the contents of her breakfast vary based on whether she's traveling or not, she makes sure to eat nutritious food.

If you regularly skip breakfast, consider changing your morning routine to include it. Indulge yourself, even if doing so means having to wake up 15 minutes earlier.

Eating healthy foods in the morning, particularly those that offer plenty of protein, will energize you and help you to focus. It'll also improve your metabolism and regulate your energy levels throughout the day.

A high-protein breakfast will also make it easier to avoid sugary snacks - for example, donuts, danishes, and candy bars. These "foods" send your blood sugar levels through the roof, inevitably setting you up for a mid-morning crash.

As for drinking coffee, I'm an advocate as long the amount of caffeine consumed is within reason. Too much caffeine can make you feel jittery, give you heartburn, cause muscle spasms, and even induce anxiety.

I consume approximately 400 milligrams of caffeine each day - 200 in the morning and 200 in the early afternoon. That's optimal for me. But I realize you and I are different. You may find that you perform better with a greater or lesser amount of caffeine in your body.

As with every practice described in this book, I encourage you to experiment with it.

- Test different volumes - for example, 200 milligrams versus 400 milligrams.
- Test different times of the day - for example, consuming all of your daily caffeine in the morning versus portioning it out throughout the morning and afternoon.
- Test different caffeinated drinks - for example, coffee versus espresso (personally, I prefer the latter).

The point is that caffeine affects each person differently. The only way to find your "sweet spot," and optimize its use is to run a few tests and monitor the effects.

Bachelder's morning routine gives her the energy and mental endurance she needs to address the challenges that accompany running a multinational fast food chain of restaurants. That's worth considering as you create your own perfect routine.

#10: RICHARD BRANSON'S "FULL THROTTLE" MORNING

~

Richard Branson is the quintessential entrepreneur. Although he heads one of the largest business entities in the world (the Virgin Group), he maintains an insatiable entrepreneurial spirit.

He started the company that would one day become the giant Virgin Group in the 1970s. Today, that company is a conglomerate that oversees more than 400 separate companies. These companies operate in a variety of sectors, from travel and entertainment to healthcare, aerospace, and communications. Branson played an instrumental role in launching nearly all of them.

Branson clearly has passion and vision. It's difficult to launch hundreds of companies and turn them into successful enterprises without possessing these traits. But passion and vision alone aren't enough to help Branson address the myriad challenges he faces throughout the day.

It's unsurprising that he considers his morning routine vital to his success.

His routine is comprised of three basic practices:

1. Wake up early
2. Exercise
3. Spend time with family

Branson wakes up at 5:00 a.m. each day. He confesses that he's been an early riser for most of his life, and attributes much of his productivity to this habit. He noted on his blog:

 "Over my 50 years in business I have learned that if I rise early I can achieve so much more in a day, and therefore in life."[1]

Once he's out of bed, he focuses on exercise. He feels physical activity not only stimulates his mind, but also gives him a massive boost of energy. He noted the following in a 2013 interview:

 "There's nothing like the endorphins from being fit, and the incredible endorphin rush that goes with that."[2]

Exercise can take on a number of different forms for Branson depending on his location and mood. On some days, he enjoys playing tennis. Other days, he prefers swimming and jogging. On still other days, he favors kitesurfing.

Following his morning exercise, Branson spends time with his family. He feels that doing so puts him in a healthy state of mind that empowers him to meet the day's business-related challenges.

Thoughts On Richard Branson's Morning Routine

As you've noticed in this section of *Morning Makeover*, many of the highly-successful people profiled here wake up early. Most of them do so to increase their productivity. Branson is no exception.

Having said that, he stresses that sleep is important, especially for those who keep a busy schedule. He noted on his blog:

 "Sleep is incredibly valuable for a busy life, and I try to get it whenever and wherever I can – especially when I'm flying."

The takeaway is that although he wakes up early each morning, he's careful not to skimp on his sleep.

In the section *Is It Necessary To Wake Up At 5:00 A.M.?*, I argued that waking up early, by itself, has little value. Being an early riser, if you choose to become one, should stem from your intentions (see the section *The Importance Of Intentionality*). You should wake up ready to take deliberate action toward your daily goals.

For Branson, being an early riser allows him to get an early start on his day. He's able to get more done than would be possible if he woke up later. Greater productivity is his intention.

Exercise is a cornerstone of Branson's morning routine. He feels it fuels both his mind and body; it sharpens his focus and makes him feel alive.

I relate to this. While I spend less time than Branson exercising in the morning, the exercise I perform fills me with energy. If you feel sluggish when you wake up, or your brain is trapped in a fog, go for a short jog. Or do 10 pushups. Or five squats. Do *something* to move your body. I'm willing to bet you'll feel more vigorous and clearheaded afterward.

Branson claims that spending time with his family in the morning puts him in a positive frame of mind. He values this effect as it helps him to deal effectively with the business of the day.

If you're not currently spending time with your spouse or

children in the morning, make an effort to do so, if only to note its effect on your attitude. I'd be willing to bet you'll feel more optimistic and confident.

Don't worry about setting aside an hour if you don't have that much time available. Even a few minutes can have a major influence on your mindset. That influence can set the tone for your entire day.

[1] https://www.virgin.com/richard-branson/why-i-wake-up-early

[2]   http://www.originmagazine.com/2013/01/15/a-conversation-with-richard-branson-by-maranda-pleasant-gina-g-murdock-and-kelly-smith/

FINAL THOUGHTS ON USING MORNING ROUTINES

~

Y ou have the power to transform your life. In the same way that your *current* circumstances are largely the result of your past decisions, your *future* circumstances will be the result of decisions you make from this point forward.

That's empowering because it means you're in control.

You get to decide how to spend your mornings. Do you want to hit snooze over and over, and eventually drag yourself from bed while feeling as if you were hit by a bus? Or do you want to spring from your bed filled with energy and passion?

Do you want to waste your morning hours watching television and hanging out on social media? Or would you rather start your mornings off right and dramatically boost your productivity?

It's entirely up to you.

If you're committed to creating morning routines that set you up for success during the day, I recommend you do two things right now.

First, write down your commitment, along with your intention, and tape it somewhere you'll see it each morning. It needn't be complicated nor eloquent. In fact, the simpler it is, the better. Here's an example:

 "I pledge to complete my morning routine today because I want to feel more relaxed."

Writing down your commitment and purpose will focus your attention and clarify what you want to achieve. Meanwhile, seeing it in written form in the morning will spur you to take action.

Second, find an accountability partner. This person's job is to hold you to your commitment. He or she will ask you daily whether you completed your morning routine. You'll be more inclined to do so if you have to report your success or failure.

After a few weeks, you'll no longer need your written commitment to serve as a trigger. Nor will you need your accountability partner. With consistent repetition, your morning routine will become an integral part of your day, similar to brushing your teeth. But in the beginning, as you adopt the habit, both practices can be invaluable.

Now's the time to decide whether you want to experience an extraordinary life, one morning at a time. You have all of the tools you need to make it happen.

I'd love to hear from you as you create, perform, and adjust your morning routines. Contact me any time to tell me about your progress and share your challenges.

DID YOU ENJOY READING MORNING MAKEOVER?

~

First, thank you so much for sticking with me throughout this book. Morning routines have had a massive influence on my productivity and mindset. My hope is that in teaching you how to create morning rituals that complement your goals, this book will improve your life in some way.

If you enjoyed reading *Morning Makeover*, would you do something for me? Would you visit Amazon and leave a quick review? It doesn't have to be long. Two or three short sentences detailing something you learned would be great!

I'm planning to publish several more action guides I think (hope) you'll love. If you'd like to hear about them before they're released, and take advantage of special discounts, consider joining my email list. As I mentioned at the beginning of the book, I'll send you my 40-page PDF ebook titled *Catapult Your Productivity! The Top 10 Habits You Must Develop To Get More Things Done* as my way of saying thanks.

You can join my list at the following address:

http://artofproductivity.com/free-gift/

I'll also share with you some of my best tips for making the most of your time, adopting new habits, and designing a truly rewarding lifestyle!

All the best,

Damon Zahariades
http://artofproductivity.com

ABOUT THE AUTHOR

Damon Zahariades is a corporate refugee who endured years of unnecessary meetings, drive-by chats with coworkers, and a distraction-laden work environment before striking out on his own. Today, in addition to being the author of a growing catalog of time management and productivity books, he's the showrunner for the productivity blog ArtofProductivity.com.

In his spare time, he shows off his copywriting chops by powering the content marketing campaigns used by today's growing businesses to attract customers.

Damon lives in Southern California with his beautiful, supportive wife and their frisky dog. He's currently staring down the barrel of his 50th birthday.

OTHER BOOKS BY DAMON ZAHARIADES

~

The Joy Of Imperfection: A Stress-Free Guide To Silencing Your Inner Critic, Conquering Perfectionism, and Becoming The Best Version Of Yourself!

Is perfectionism causing you to feel stressed, irritated, and chronically unhappy? Here's how to silence your inner critic, embrace imperfection, and live without fear!

~

The Art Of Saying NO: How To Stand Your Ground, Reclaim Your Time And Energy, And Refuse To Be Taken For Granted (Without Feeling Guilty!)

Are you fed up with people taking you for granted? Learn how to set boundaries, stand your ground, and inspire others' respect in the process!

~

The Procrastination Cure: 21 Proven Tactics For Conquering Your Inner Procrastinator, Mastering Your Time, And Boosting Your Productivity!

Do you struggle with procrastination? Discover how to take quick action, make fast decisions, and finally overcome your inner procrastinator!

～

Fast Focus: A Quick-Start Guide To Mastering Your Attention, Ignoring Distractions, And Getting More Done In Less Time!

Are you constantly distracted? Does your mind wander after just a few minutes? Learn how to develop laser-sharp focus!

～

Small Habits Revolution: 10 Steps To Transforming Your Life Through The Power Of Mini Habits!

Got 5 minutes a day? Use this simple, effective plan for creating any new habit you desire!

～

To-Do List Formula: A Stress-Free Guide To Creating To-Do Lists That Work!

Finally! A step-by-step system for creating to-do lists that'll actually help you to get things done!

～

The 30-Day Productivity Plan: Break The 30 Bad Habits That Are Sabotaging Your Time Management - One Day At A Time!

Need a daily action plan to boost your productivity? This 30-day guide is the solution to your time management woes!

～

The Time Chunking Method: A 10-Step Action Plan For Increasing

Your Productivity

It's one of the most popular time management strategies used today. Double your productivity with this easy 10-step system.

~

Digital Detox: The Ultimate Guide To Beating Technology Addiction, Cultivating Mindfulness, and Enjoying More Creativity, Inspiration, And Balance In Your Life!

Are you addicted to Facebook and Instagram? Are you obsessed with your phone? Use this simple, step-by-step plan to take a technology vacation!

For a complete list, please visit

http://artofproductivity.com/my-books/

16041118R00089